THE WASTE OF NATIONS

An argument for the absolute necessity of reconversion and optimization of displaced resources and the development of new concepts in planetary economic management to protect the earth's dwindling water supply, ensure adequate resources to accommodate population growth, and cut back on overuse of chemical fertilizers.

THE WASTE
OF
NATIONS

The Economic Utilization of
Human Waste in Agriculture

LATTEE A. FAHM

ALLANHELD, OSMUN Montclair

ALLANHELD, OSMUN & CO. PUBLISHERS, INC.
Montclair, New Jersey

Published in the United States of America in 1980
by Allanheld, Osmun & Co., 19 Brunswick Road, Montclair, N.J. 07042
and by Universe Books, 381 Park Avenue South, New York 10016
Distribution: Universe Books

LIBRARY OF CONGRESS CATALOGING IN PUBLICATION DATA

Fahm, Lattee A
   The waste of nations.

   Includes index.
   1. Night soil.   2.   Fertilizers and manures.
3. Agriculture.   4.   Food supply.   I.   Title.
S657.F34   338.4'7'66863   79-88260
ISBN 0-916672-28-X

printed in the United States of America

*To the memory of my Father
and for Mother, Carolyn, and Fauzi*

CONTENTS

Tables and Figures

xi

Abbreviations Used in Text

CoR	Club of Rome
CRC	Chemical Rubber Company
EPA	Environmental Protection Agency
ERS	Economic Research Service
FAO	Food and Agricultural Organization of the United Nations
IAEA	International Atomic Energy Agency
IBRD	International Bank for Reconstruction and Development (World Bank)
ICAR	Indian Council on Agricultural Research
IIASA	International Institute for Applied Systems Analysis
ISMA	International Superphosphate Manufacturers Association
LDC	Less Developed Countries
NPK	Nitrogen Phosphate Potassium Fertilizers
NRC	National Research Council
OECD	Organization for Economic Cooperation and Development
OXFAM	Oxford Committee for Famine Relief
R&D	Research and Development
SSSA	Soil Science Society of America
TVA	Tennessee Valley Authority
UNEP	United Nations Environmental Program
UNDP	United Nations Development Program
UNIDO	United Nations Industrial Development Organization
UNITAR	United Nations Institute for Training and Research
USDA	United States Department of Agriculture
VID	Vienna Institute for Development
WHO	World Health Organization
WMO	World Meteorological Organization

PREFACE

This book is about the high costs of wastefulness. Although not intended to be a detailed treatment of localized problems, it discusses the ecological relation of human waste to population, food, and energy levels in the global flow of material processes and transformations. The book also considers the social circumstances in which an enormous quantity of valuable nutrients trapped in human waste goes unreclaimed despite the world's chronic deficiency of agronutrients needed for food production.

The essential difference between this book and others dealing with similar problems is that the former departs from the traditional approach by putting primary emphasis on a unified global solution: it presents an integrative view of a process in which the human waste is transformed into agronutrients required by plants and animals on which mankind depends for food and energy. It calls for the formation of a Global Authority on Waste Elimination and Reconversion—under the UN—to coordinate necessary national programs and to promote, induce, and accelerate the development of socially and technologically optimal reconversion systems for primary waste. The program envisaged would facilitate and ultimately secure (a) the transformation of human waste into agronutrients and related products commanding positive exchange values and social utility, and (b) the effective and productive reabsorption of recovered agronutrients in socio-ecosystems. Unfortunately, a powerful combination of factors is at work in the contemporary world opposed to the types of solutions envisaged, factors which include conventional prejudice and atavistic superstition toward human waste. In addition, neither the necessity for nor the feasibility of a solution based on the population-food-waste relationship is recognized. The basic obstacles must be cleared first, in order to deal effectively with problems of body waste management at the local level.

In this study, the consideration of practical applications of nutrients recoverable from body waste has been confined to the field of agriculture. It will be shown in subsequent chapters that the control, containment, and final resolution of the supply of food and agronutrients will result in a combination of short- and long-term goals: in the short run, to contain and ameliorate deprivation and suffering caused by maldistribution of material goods; in the long run, to expand food and fertilizer production worldwide and, in particular, to increase production capabilities in less-developed countries. The ultimate objective is to help involve more people and communities in the maintenance of global control and eventual elimination of world food and commodity shortages. In the special case of catastrophic emergencies, massive global transfers or redistribution of resources are urgently required. In such conditions that normally result from disruptive and paralyzing effects of man or nature, material relief through redistribution of resources alone can achieve only limited global success. In recognition of the interplay of some of the elements comprising the short-run and long-run measures, it is important to ensure not only that their dynamic effects are mutually reenforcing, but also that the total sum does sustain the tangible goals sought at local and global levels.

The discussions are conveniently organized into four sections: Part I presents the *Prologue*, Part II reviews the

Problems, Part III examines the *Prospects*, and Part IV outlines the *Programs*. The first two chapters of Part I describe the elements of certain key global issues—including world population, agricultural production, and world food supply—in geographic and historical contexts of the post-World War II period. The implications of the underlying trends for the remainder of this century are duly noted. Part II is devoted to the development and discussion of analytical concepts: the food-energy-waste relation, the coefficient of gross assimilation of food substances, the potential dangers of human body waste at the global level, and other related topics. Ideas of pivotal interest concerning material recovery, economic valuation, and utilization of human waste are discussed in various sections of Part III. Estimates of the material and economic values of agronutrients recoverable from body waste are presented. The data for the year 1975 are disaggregated for special evaluation. In anticipation of future developments, the projection of trends to 2000 A.D. is evaluated against the background of developments in the last 25 years. The last four chapters in Part IV present the concluding discussions. The first two are an assessment of the crucial function of fertilizers in the world's agricultural production function. The final sections consider the global necessity, as well as the possibilities, of recovering and utilizing the chemical constituents of human waste.

The following points concerning the conceptual limits of this study should be noted. First, certain empirical issues of local interest, including those arising from the choice of techniques and from engineering designs of prototype equipment, will be discussed only in reference to a few countries. Such topics as the availability of equipment, data on soil composition, climatic patterns, hydrological structure, urban-rural demographic balance, and viability of prevailing agricultural organization lie beyond the limits of this volume. A second book covering these aspects is at the planning stage.

Kenneth Boulding has foretold, in his "Ballad of Ecological Awareness," the coming of a brand new "expert"—the poleconecologist—whose duties will include, presumably, giving real attention to the value of the Gross National Waste of countries. When that happens, the Gross National Products of countries, as presently constituted, will never be the same again!

Berkeley, California, 1979

ACKNOWLEDGMENTS

This book owes much to a number of individuals as well as to the international developments and activities to which I devoted some attention while on assignment at the United Nation's Institute for Training and Research (UNITAR). It is impossible to acknowledge every individual deserving credit for stimulating this research. In particular, I am indebted to Dr. Davidson Nicol, executive director of UNITAR, and to Dr. Aurelio Peccei, president of the Club of Rome (CoR). While at UNITAR, my views on the subject were discussed with colleagues at the Food and Agriculture Organization (FAO), World Bank (IBRD), United Nations Environmental Program (UNEP), United Nations Environmental Program (UNEP), United Nations Development Program (UNDP), United Nations Industrial Development Organization (UNIDO), International Institute for Applied Systems Analysis (IIASA), and Vienna Institute for Development (VID). I have also benefited from exchanging views on related subjects with, among others, Professors A. Schultz, S. Margin, and H. Linnemann; Drs. N. Hetzer, Y. Maxon, P. Buringh, H. van Heemst, F. Rabar, and Jan van Ettinger, director of the project "Reshaping the International Order," none of whom share my full and total responsibility for the views and opinions expressed in this book. The University of California library facilities, especially the Agricultural Library at Berkeley, provided an invaluable support for the necessary research, for which I am grateful. Many thanks to Tiqui Salvado and Sherrie Yeung for their highly efficient and indispensable secretarial assistance. Finally, my special thanks to Mr. Matthew Held, my publisher, for raising and discussing a number of important questions prompted by his critical and constructive reading of the manuscript.

L. A. Fahm

THE WASTE OF NATIONS

INTRODUCTION

A sound man is good at salvage,
At seeing nothing is lost.

Lao Tze, 500 B.C.

The basic methods of human body waste disposal in effect around the world include burying, burning, and water borne systems and are a combination of techniques some of which were adopted more than two millennia ago. Among the existing processes, the sewage system—an integrated program of collection, treatment and disposal of body waste, based on water carriage—represents the most advanced public sanitation engineering practice to have evolved over the past hundred years.

Suppose for a moment that a hypothetical Planetary Sewage Treatment Authority were to mandate that this standard process of waste treatment be applied uniformly as a worldwide system. What would be the probable global impact of such a program? At best, a worldwide sewage treatment program would (a) minimize the squalor and fetid nuisance seeping from cesspools, outhouses, and open gutters in many parts of the world; (b) significantly destroy dangerous bacteria living in body (primary) waste; and (c) appreciably raise the average standard of public health. Despite these desirable results, a universal modern sewage treatment program would not be able to solve the problem of waste-free conservational disposal of body waste, and the long-term ecological impact of the accumulation of waste by-products from processing facilities would be unfavorable, if not dangerous, to public health. Moreover, the magnitude of global resources needed for such a program would be prohibitively large. It takes between 1,000 and 2,000 tons of water at various stages of the process to flush one ton of solid body waste. In a future world community of more than five billion people, for example, producing a conservatively estimated one million metric tons of body waste daily, the volume of water needed, for this plus other essential water requirements, would be extremely difficult, if not impossible, to provide on a steady basis. The water supply in some parts of the world has already reached such critical levels that conservation programs are urgently needed to reduce world water consumption by at least one third and to develop new and more efficient methods of replenishing our global freshwater supply.

As long as the central problem of body waste reconversion remains unsolved, the future ecological situation is likely to become progressively worse with the growth in number and size of cities and urban centers. Although most sewer transport arteries and processing installations are already concentrated in large cities in developed countries, it is not unusual for some of these communities, like New York or Paris, to discharge from 30 to 50 percent of their untreated sewage into surrounding waters, especially during the rainy season. In rural areas of developed countries, however, sewage treatment facilities are, at best, limited and marginal. Most rural communities depend on varying combinations of sewers and septic tanks supplemented, on occasion, by outhouse facilities. In view of the inherent limitations of conventional body waste treatment facilities, the problem of treatment and disposal is more than an academic question.

The problem of body waste management in developing countries is even more serious. The typical method of handling human body waste in an underdeveloped country is not only more dangerous, potentially, but has consistently undermined local efforts to establish better standards of public health. In most developing nations, urban areas are served by an extensive network of pit holes, septic tanks, and an occasional sewage treatment installation. With due allowances for exceptional cases, it is safe to say that in the underdeveloped world at large, sewage transport and processing facilities are available only to a very limited and marginal extent. Sanitation engineers conversant with local situations feel that modern body waste treatment and handling facilities are so limited (on the average, about 5 percent of total body waste output is handled by sewage treatment, 30 percent by septic tanks, and about 50 percent by cesspools and outhouses) that local standards of public sanitation are well below modern models.

New ideas and designs are needed which will transform human body waste into material resources that can be absorbed by the socio-ecosystem. One such possibility is in the area of agronutrients—the production of plant and soil nutrients. Given the magnitude of projected global demands for plant-foods for the next 20 years (estimated in hundreds of millions metric tons), and the progressively sharp increase in the costs and hazards of conventional fertilizers, to mobilize the material constituents of human body waste for plant nutrients would, if successful, permanently increase the material basis of social and economic progress for all mankind. In a pioneering sense, the reclamation of soil and plant nutrients from body waste is a basic program in the long-range goal of planetary resource management and conservation. The operational idea behind the proposed method of solution is simple: to eliminate the age-old problem of disposal by turning primary human waste into valuable agricultural inputs. The tangible advantages to be realized (i.e., potential savings in the rate of conventional fertilizer use) would increase as the production of plant nutrients from body waste increase. Other potential benefits would include a reduction in the levels of ground and subsurface water pollution (the waste products of conventional sewage treatment) and improved maintenance and enhancement of the amenity of community waters.

Henceforth, new models of human designs for living must assume a global, rather than national, perspective. Our future survival and the quality of human life will depend increasingly on man's ability to learn that the resources of his planet must be efficiently utilized, scrupulously recycled, prudently conserved, and equitably redistributed. It is abundantly clear that new systems must be designed to eliminate the enormous losses and uncontrolled leakages of energy and other resources which occur in socio-ecosystems. The failure of the world community to control and productively manage the global flow of body waste is one example of our wasteful indifference to and imprudent neglect of the "displaced resources." This neglect we pay for dearly by accelerating the pollution and degradation of human environments.

PART I: PROLOGUE: World Population, Agricultural Production, and Food Supply in the Postwar Economy

1

POPULATION, FOOD, AND ECONOMIC DISPLACEMENTS

> If after the political, economic, and financial experiences of recent years we still think that states, however proud and independent they may feel, can go it alone in these matters, ignoring each other's interests and above all the interests of the impoverished and backward states, then we are beyond redemption.
>
> Lester B. Pearson, *Reshaping the International Order**

Mankind has reached a critical turning point in the evolution of postwar political and economic order. At this present juncture, a combination of worldwide climatic, biological, and institutional displacements has effected fundamental shifts in the structure of the world economy, particularly the world food and energy situation.[1] With regard to the production of food grains, the question being asked, even in developed countries, is how much longer the favorable postwar experience of the rising output per hectare will last. The steady supply of "cheap energy" and the permissive technology it fostered was as

*New York: E.P. Dutton, 1976, p. 59.

indispensable to the postwar boom in agriculture and food production as it was to the postwar global energy crisis which began in 1972 and marked the beginning of the end of the postwar trend in agricultural development. As one of the direct effects of the energy crisis, a growing shortage of fertilizers and other related farm inputs appeared. During the worst interval of the crisis, most countries were seriously threatened with mass starvation and internal political and economic chaos. This was especially true of the developing countries, the majority of the world population.

In 1975 the population was conservatively estimated at 4.2 billion,[2] two-thirds of whom inhabited the developing world. During the preceding 25 years, world population had increased by more than 1.5 billion people. If present trends continue, by 2000 A.D. the population will rise by more than 2.5 billion people. On the basis of postwar population behavior, the expected level in 1985 is at least twice as large as 1950 (i.e., 2,486 million people). At its current rate of increase, world population will reach about 8.5 billion by the end of the first decade of the twenty-first century. It is sobering to note that this projected population is more than double that in 1975. The stark reality of population behavior engenders widespread concern once again about the Malthusian specter.[3] In retrospect—and with particular reference to the 1972–1975 famine—the measures adopted by bilateral and multilateral agencies to prevent the greater part of mankind from chronic starvation were extraordinarily inadequate, burdensome, and profoundly demoralizing. It is important to realize, in this connection, that the world has never before fed as many as 5 billion people. In the wake of the twenty-first century, there could be thousands of millions more people to feed. Judged by our contemporary experience, the inevitable crisis generated by feeding such a congregation of people could be virtually unmanageable and ultimately disastrous for mankind.

In technical language, the world food problem may be described as the cumulative effects of structural disequilibria between the underlying global food supply and population

generating functions.[4] The interacting elements of the phenomena have produced social crisis and catastrophe manifested
most severely in certain geopolitical areas of the world.[5] For
example, in the first half of the twentieth century, it was
estimated that one out of three persons went to bed hungry.
Today, the ratio is two out of three,[6] and by the twenty-first
century, it may be three out of four. The probable outcome of
this race between food supply and human population is a
prolonged state of neo-Malthusian disequilibrium.[7]

It is relevant to review some pertinent historical facts about
the world food supply. From 1950 to 1970 the combined output
of edible crops and animal products increased by more than
twofold. Over the same period, world population increased
only by 50 percent, from 2.4 billion to 3.6 billion. With regard
to the aggregate demand and global distribution of the food
products, however, 70 percent of the twofold increase was
absorbed by the developed countries (i.e., by less than one-third
of the world population) while the remaining 30 percent went
to the developing countries (i.e., to more than two-thirds of the
world population). Whichever way one may look at it, the
international mechanisms for food allocation operated consistently to preserve the underlying inequities in global food
distribution.[8] In letter and spirit, the law of distribution has
conformed more to the mandate of Matthew the publican than
to that of Jesus the Christ.

Between 1972 and 1975, food production and distribution
systems were badly disrupted by an assortment of economic and
political crises. In a relatively short time, the volatile behavior
of the unfolding phenomena had escalated into acute instability of the world economy. In retrospect, the year 1972 marks a
turning point in the propagation of the new trends. Judging
from the cautious and responsive stance of the business
community, most technical observers agree that the "abrupt
transition of the world food economy from a buyer's market . . .
as well as the consequent rise in food prices, was not widely
anticipated. Between late 1972 and 1973, the world price of
wheat tripled, and the price of rice followed. Soybean prices

doubled in a twenty-four month period."[9] As market stability weakened in wild speculation, world market transactions heated up under an unprecedented grip of uncertainty. The sparks of inflation already kindled by the sudden increase in food prices were fed by an equally dramatic rise in petroleum prices; within a few weeks, the commodity markets were set ablaze under an explosive triple digit inflation in the world prices of oil, basic metals, and food. In the circumstances, the national and international position of many countries changed drastically, mostly for the worst, although a few oil- and food-exporting countries benefited substantially from the international economic crisis.

An assessment of the total impact of the economic displacements indicates that the "poorer countries importing both food and oil suffered the greatest damage. The many countries having no valuable raw material of their own to export exhausted their limited foreign exchange reserves in a matter of months, and several were on the verge of international bankruptcy."[10] The impact on developing countries was the most severe. For example, in 1973 between 0.4 and 0.5 billion children suffered from malnutrition and starvation, according to FAO, UNESCO, and UNICEF estimates.[11] In addition, hundreds of millions of adults were also victims, and many could not maintain their capacity to work because of deficient diet.[12] It is demoralizing to note that even optimistic forecasts do not offer any hope for significant improvement. According to authoritative sources, "world food demand in the seventies and eighties is calculated to grow at a rate of 2.4 percent per annum, of which 2 percent represents population increase and 0.4 percent increased purchasing power."[13] In 1970, for example, the world food demand was about 2.6 billion metric tons. By 1985, the FAO expects world consumption to rise by 40 percent to about 3.7 billion metric tons.[14] Based on an optimistic assessment of the situation, it is also expected that "there would still be in 1985 some 34 countries with a combined population of 800 million in which, because of the continuing poverty, effective demand for food would still fall short of food energy requirements."[15]

With the exception of man's everpresent anxiety of self-destruction by his nuclear arsenals, observers believe that the long-term behavior of our food supply in relation to population growth ranks among the most crucial determinants of future world political and economic stability.[16] In the light of recent displacements (1972–75) which occurred in the prevailing food supply trend, the conventional wisdom is that the world community has no other acceptable choice but to adopt all the measures necessary to increase food production as expeditiously as possible. If global efforts prove successful, mankind may be able to prevent the recurrence of the 1972–74 famine and even more catastrophic political and economic instability in the waning years of the present century. Such an assignment, however, seems almost impossible in the context of present realities. It is quite evident that the supply side of food production is becoming increasingly tight.[17] In effect, the basic resources required to produce more food—land, energy, fertilizers, water—are becoming increasingly scarce. In these circumstances, an increase in fertilizer inputs—the decisive factor in the postwar agricultural miracles—may yet offer the best hope and the widest substitution possibility among the agricultural factors of production. From the earliest times, students of soil sciences have been aware of the latent possibilities in the whole field of organic fertilizers.[18] In this area alone (and perhaps, to the same extent, in the inorganic fields as well) there are alternate sources of plant nutrients that are still insufficiently researched and engineered. The time has come for an unfettered program of research and development, and the *activation* of those latent possibilities; it is time to shake off sterile conventionalism and become bold and innovative in response to the manifest needs of suffering humanity.

In agriculture, as in other food production processes, it is a fundamental law that more inputs are required to produce more output. The magnitude of the food supply necessary to prevent potential famine in the remainder of this century will be unattainable unless a greatly expanded supply of fertilizers, offered at lower-than-usual prevailing prices, is available to farmers in developing countries. Such an event is unlikely to occur in the normal context of the world fertilizer market since (a) basic resources utilized in commercial fertilizers are nonrenewable and therefore relatively scarce,[19] and (b) the energy content of the production processes is extremely high and costly. As a result of the inflation in the energy and resource markets, future prices of commercial fertilizers are expected to be even higher than they are at present.[20] Based on the allocative functions of the international market mechanisms alone, whether at current or future prices it is virtually impossible to satisfy the enormous fertilizer needs of the farmers in the developing countries who are primarily responsible for feeding some 70 percent of the world population. To the extent that the prevailing market mechanisms for adjusting supply and demand for food and fertilizers remain impersonal, it would require the intervention of the usual types of antihuman controls such as starvation, disease, and death to adjust the world food demand to the world food supply.

One alternative to this dismal prospect involves the development of synthetic organic nutrients (fertilizers) such as body waste manure to supplement the total supply of synthetic inorganic nutrients (commercial fertilizers). It is crucial that man review the global implications of every major conventional and unconventional source of fertilizers to promote the appropriate total response to ecological transformations of matter and conservation of energy in our planetary system. Undoubtedly, the time has come to shed the timid, half-hearted, and partisan tendencies that may hinder the concentration of research and development efforts in the search for new sources of fertilizers.

NOTES

1. The various aspects of "world problematique," as well as the solutions prescribed, do reveal certain inherent contradictions stemming from the diverse windows of observations. For example, see and compare the following: UN, *Declarations and Program of Action on the Establishment of a New International Order*, DESI.E 21 (New York, 1974); UN, *Resolutions on Development and International Economic Cooperation*, #3362, 7th Special Session of the General Assembly (New York, 1975); M. Mesarovic and E. Pestel, *Mankind at the Turning Point*, 2nd Report to the Club of Rome (New York: E.P. Dutton, 1974); J. Tinbergen, *Reshaping the International Order*, A Report to the Club of Rome (New York: E.P. Dutton, 1976); W. Leontieff, *The Future of the World Economy*, A Study Sponsored by the United Nations. Doc. ST/ESA/44 (New York, 1976); H. Linnemann, *MOIRA: Model of International Relations in Agriculture* (Amsterdam: North Holland Pub. Co., 1976); Ervin Laszlo et al., *Goals for Mankind* (New York: E.P. Dutton, 1977).

2. The Environmental Fund, *World Population Estimates* (Washington, D.C.: 1975); UN *Demographic Yearbook*, Annual (New York, 1975).

3. T. R. Malthus, *First Essay on Population* (London: Macmillan & Co., 1966), pp. 11–17; Lord Walston, *Dealing with Hunger* (London: The Bodley Head, 1976), pp. 42–56.

4. D. S. Halacy, Jr., *The Geometry of Hunger* (New York: Harper & Row, 1972), chapter 1.

5. J. D. Tydings, *Born to Starve* (New York: William Morrow & Co., 1970), pp. 3–94.

6. H. de Castro, *The Geography of Hunger* (Boston: Little, Brown & Co., 1952), p. 4ff.

7. R. McNamara, *One Hundred Countries, Two Billion People: The Dimensions of Development* (New York: Praeger, 1973), pp. 19–48; Mesarovic and Pestel, op. cit., p. 115ff.

8. H. de Castro, *The Black Book of Hunger* (New York: Funk & Wagnalls, 1967), pp. 5–20; R. Reville, "Food and Population," *Scientific American* 231 no. 3 (September 1974).

9. L. R. Brown, *By Bread Alone* (New York: Praeger, 1974), p. 4; L. P. Shertz, "World Food: Prices and Poor," *Foreign Affairs* 52 no. 3 (April 1974).

10. L. R. Brown, op. cit., p. 5.

11. Mesarovic and Pestel, op. cit., p. 115; UN *Assessment of the World Food Situation*, E/Conf/65/3 (1974), p. 5.

11. H. de Castro, *The Black Book of Hunger*, p. 12; FAO, *Lives in Peril: Protein and the Child*, Protein Advisory Group (Rome, 1970); FAO/WHO, *Energy and Protein Requirements*, Report of Ad Hoc Expert Committee (Rome, 1973), UN, *Assessment of the World Food Situation*, pp. 5–6.

13. UN, Assessment of the World Food Situation, p. 6; USDA, *The World Food Situation and Prospects to 1985* (Washington: Economic Research Service, 1974), pp. 32–40.

14. FAO, *Preliminary Mid-Term Review and Appraisal*, FAO/DD2/75/2 (Rome: March, 1975), pp. 40–44.

15. Ibid., pp. 42–43; Mesarovic and Pestel, op. cit., chapter 9; UN, *Assessment of the World Food Situation*, pp. 6–7, 85–86.

16. L. R. Brown, op. cit., pp. 58–72; Messarovic and Pestel, op. cit., pp. 56–69, 115–129; P. H. Abelson, ed. "Food: Politics, Economics, Nutrition and Research," *Science* Special Compendium (1975), p. 57; D. H. and D. L. Meadows, J. Randers, and W. W. Behrens III, *The Limits to Growth* (London: Earth Island Press, 1972), chapter 2; D. Jones, *Food and Interdependence* (London: UK Overseas Development Institute, 1976); Lord Walston, op. cit., pp. 9–12, 25–41.

17. G. D. Johnson, *World Food Problems and Prospects* (Washington: American Enterprise Institute, 1973), pp. 49–50; FAO, *State of Food and Agriculture* (Rome, 1974), p. 32, (1975), chapter 1; President's Science Advisory Committee, *The World Food Problem* (Washington: GPO, 1967), pp. 83–90; *Fertilizers in Retrospect and Prospect*, Proc. of the Fertilizer Society 121 (London, 1963); Gregory Scmid, "Investment Opportunities in Food Production in LDC's" in *Food Policy* (May 1976): 220–231; Lord Walston, op. cit., pp. 42–69; J. C. Meisner, "Food or Famine for the Future," *Agricultural Economics Papers*, Department of Economics (Columbia, Missouri: University of Missouri, 1975).

18. P. M. Cato and M. T. Varro, *On Agriculture*, ed. T. D. Page (Cambridge, Mass.: Harvard University Press, 1960), 263–265; FAO, *Organic Materials as Fertilizers*, Soils Bulletin 27 (Rome, 1975), pp. 19–31; A. C. Garg, M. A. Idani, T. P. Abraham, *Organic Manures* (New Delhi: Indian Council of Agricultural Research, 1971), pp. 2–14; Sir Albert Howard, *An Agricultural Testament* (London: Oxford University Press, 1940), chapter 7; Sir Albert Howard, *The Soil and Health* (New York: Devin-Adair Press, 1947), chapters 4, 12 and 13; M. M. Kononova, *Soil Organic Matter* 2nd ed. (New York: Pergamon Press, 1966), pp. 46–50; A. I. Mackay, *Farming and Gardening in the Bible* (Emmaus, Pennsylvania: Rodale Press, 1950), pp. 203–206; FAO, *Organic Materials and Soil Productivity*, Soils Bulletin 35 (Rome, 1977).

19. L. R. Brown, op. cit., pp. 114–130; TVA, *World Fertilizer Market Review and Outlook* (Muscle Shoals, Alabama, 1974), p. 104ff; USDA, *World Fertilizer Review and Prospects to 1980/81* (Washington: Economic Research Service, 1974); FAO "Long Term Fertilizer Supply/Demand Position and Elements of World Fertilizer Policy," AGS F/75/77 (Rome, 1975).

20. G. W. Ames, "Fertilizer Price Inflation: A Threat to Green Revolution," *American Journal of Agricultural Economics* 57 no. 5 (1975): p. 978; *Fertilizer News* 20 no. 12, Proc. of International Superphosphate and Compound Manufacturers' Assn. (December 1975): 3–12 and 20–26; also see note 19 above.

FURTHER READING

Ardrey, Robert. *The Territorial Imperative*. New York: Atheneum, 1966.

Aziz, S. *Hunger Politics and Markets. The Real Issues in the Food Crisis*. New York: New York University Press, 1975.

Bechst, J. E., and Belzung, L. D. *World Resource Management*. Englewood Cliffs, N.J.: Prentice-Hall, 1975.

Boulding, Kenneth. "The Economics of the Coming Spaceship Earth," in *Environmental Quality in a Growing Economy*, edited by H. Jarret. Baltimore: Johns Hopkins Press, 1966.

Cohen, Mark N. *The Food Crisis in Prehistory*. New Haven: Yale University Press, 1977.

Dorfman, R., and Dorfman, N. S., eds. *Economics of the Environment*. New York: W.W. Norton & Co., 1972.

Dumond, René, and Rosier, B. *The Hungry Future*. New York: F.A. Praeger, 1969.

Eckholm, Eric. *Losing Ground: Environmental Stress and World Food Prospects*. New York: W.W. Norton & Co., 1976.

Forrester, J. *World Dynamics*. Cambridge, Mass.: Wright-Allen Press, 1971.

Freeman, Orville. *World Without Hunger*. New York: F.A. Praeger, 1968.

George, Susan. *How the Other Half Dies*. Montclair, N.J.: Allanheld, Osmun & Co., 1977.

Gibbon, John. *Forecasts, Famines, and Freezes: Climate & Man's Future*. New York: Walker & Co., 1976.

Habakkuk, A. J. *Population Growth and Economic Development Since 1750*. Leicester, England: Leicester Univ. Press, 1972.

Helmann, Hal. *Feeding the World of the Future*. New York: M. Evans & Co., 1972.

Kay, D. A., and Skolnikoff, E. B. *World Eco-crisis: International Organizations in Response*. Madison: Univ. of Wisconsin, 1976.

Lappe, Francis M. *Food First, Beyond the Myth of Scarcity*. Boston: Houghton Mifflin Co., 1977.

Linneman, H., *MOIRA: Model of International Relations in Agriculture*. Amsterdam: North Holland Publ. Co., 1976.

Lucas, J. *Our Polluted Food*. New York: John Wiley & Sons, 1974.

Mullick, M. A. H. "The Present Food Crisis: A Plaidoyer for Developing Food Potential in the Third World," in *Economia Internationale*. 28 (3/4) (1975), pp. 430–452.

The Nutrition Foundation, Inc. *Food, Science and Society*, Berkeley, Calif.: The Nutrition Foundation, Inc., 1968.

Paddock, W. *Hungry Nations*. Boston: Little, Brown & Co., 1964.

———. *Famine 1975*. Boston: Little, Brown & Co., 1967.

Pearce, D. W., ed. *the Economics of Natural Resource Depletion*. New York: John Wiley & Sons, 1975.

Pearson, F. A., and Harper, F. A. *The World's Hunger*. Ithaca, N.Y.: Cornell University Press, 1945.

Perelman, Michael. *Farming for Profit in a Hungry World*. Montclair, N.J.: Allanheld, Osmun & Co., 1977.

Phillips, J. *The Development of Agriculture and Forestry in the Tropics*. London: Faber & Faber, 1961.

Pirie, N. W. *Food Resources, Conventional and Novel*. Baltimore: Penguin Books, 1969.

Ricker, J. H. "Food from the Sea," in *Resources and Man*, P. E. Cloud, Jr., ed. New York: W.H. Freeman & Co., 1969.

Rockefeller Foundation. *Toward the Conquest of Hunger Progress Report*. 1956–66. New York, 1967.

Salk, Jonas. *Survival of the Wisest*. New York: Harper & Row, 1973.

Schurr, S. H., ed. *Energy, Economic Growth and the Environment*. Baltimore: Johns Hopkins Press, 1972.

Slesser, M. "How Many Can We Feed?" in *Ecologist* 6 (1973).

UN. *A New UN Structure for Global Economic Cooperation*, E/AC 62/9. May 1975.

UN. *A Report of the Second General Conference of the UNIDO*, A/10112 (Lima Declaration and Plan of Action on Industrial Development and Cooperation). June, 1975.

UNEP/UNCTAD. Proceedings of Cocoyoc Symposium on Patterns of Resource Use, Environment and Development Strategies, 1975 (particularly the Cocoyoc Declaration).

Walston, Lord. *Dealing with Hunger*. London: The Bodley Head, 1976.

Ward, B., & Dubos, Rene. *Only One Earth*. Hammondsworth, England: Penguin books, 1972.

Zurhorst, C. *The Conservation Fraud*. New York: Cowles Book Co., 1966.

2

AGRICULTURE AND
WORLD FOOD SUPPLY

Population, when unchecked, increases in a geometri-
cal ratio. Subsistence increases only in an arithmetical
ratio. A slight acquaintance with numbers will show the
immensity of the first power as compared with the
second.

T. R. Malthus,
*An Essay on the Principle of Population**

Most observers agree that agricultural modernization on a
worldwide scale is a necessary step in solving the food
problem.[1] During the past five years, the prices of agricultural
inputs—land, water, energy and fertilizer[2]—have risen and
caused production costs to increase faster than at any other time
in the postwar period. After 1950, productivity per hectare rose
faster than relative factor costs in the developed economies
generally, and also in some selected developing countries.[3] But
since 1971, the favorable difference between rising agricultural
productivity and resource costs has diminished drastically due,

*London, 1798, pp. 6–8.

among other factors, to the combined effects of prolonged drought, the energy crisis, and the secular denudation of soil fertility. Already, a substantial number of small farmers in underdeveloped economies—and, to a limited extent, in developed economies as well—has been forced out of agriculture by the substantial increases in resource costs. In the light of these events, the already limited contributions of developing countries to world food supply will probably decline further in future critical years unless the small farmers are provided adequate supplies of energy and fertilizers on a concessionary basis.

In formulating a corrective program to increase world food production, one traditional method is to expand the area under cultivation. The main factors preventing world agricultural production—especially edible crops and animal products—from achieving optimal levels are not only the global scarcity of prime arable land and fertilizer, but also the global techno-cultural limitations prevalent in contemporary agricultural practice. In other words, the severity of underlying technical and organizational imperfections in agricultural practice prevent the international equalization of opportunities for efficient technical adaptation in agriculture.[4] Thus it would appear that most conventional types of aid to boost farm production in developing countries would make only a marginal difference because the types of action programs being prescribed for those needy countries fall far short of what is required at the global level to institute successfully a comprehensive modernization of agricultural production. Finally, looking beyond the critical needs of present-day agricultural production, it is also necessary to anticipate and assess carefully the probable realities of future agriculture and food supply problems in a planetary sense.

With regard to the prevailing techno-cultural mode of agricultural practice in different parts of the world, one finds that the wide range of variation in productivity per hectare in yields of food crops, such as wheat, rice, and maise, is far beyond the range of statistical errors of measurements. For example, during 1969-1971 the differential in crop production between certain representative sample's of developed and developing countries are as follows: wheat—more than 3 metric tons per hectare; rice—more than 4 metric tons per hectare; and maize—more than 4 metric tons per hectare.[5] These productivity differentials suggest, among other things, the need for an international mechanism to equalize opportunities through efficient adaptation of technology in the whole field of agriculture. With appropriate modification of present conditions, the prevailing output of wheat, rice, and maize per hectare in developing countries can be increased up the three hundred, perhaps four hundred, percent. Suppose the choice of technique to increase food production in the developing countries were between (a) the expansion of area presently under cultivation, and (b) the equalization of opportunities through efficient technological adaptations on land presently under cultivation. Relevant input-output data prove that the efficiency of the latter alternative would be, on the average, about three times greater than the former, everything else being equal.[6]

The purpose of the present discussion is not to demonstrate the superiority of one method of production over another but to point out the range of potential bargains from practically adaptable agricultural techniques available to developing countries. Given the prevailing trends of world population and food supplies, it is abundantly clear that any practical method of agricultural modernization that could triple the contributions of developing countries to the world food supply would help to stem the rising tide of global hunger and starvation.[7] Although it would be quite unrealistic to expect dramatic achievements in the short run, it is not unreasonable to expect, from an effective long-term campaign, a net gain of 25 to 50 percent of the average yield per hectare in wheat, rice and maize which prevails in developing countries. With an estimated area of about 1.6 billion hectares of land under global agricultural production, the corresponding magnitude of potential gains in crop yields could run into hundreds of millions of metric tons of additional supplies of food annually. In addition, a complementary campaign to raise the crop yields in the developed world by at least one ton per hectare should be launched simultaneously to help eradicate world hunger.

The search for adequate responses to some of the given challenges must be accelerated. In the following chapters, we review a dynamic process in which the explosive population growth, limited food supply possibilities, and the potential bargain from the ascending global flow of human body waste are interconnected. The recovery of agronutrients from human waste is viewed as an indispensable multipurpose global measure to achieve:

(a) worldwide mobilization of abundant, nonconventional, energy-efficient fertilizer resources;

(b) the elimination of global agricultural underdevelopment due to chronic underconsumption of fertilizers by the majority of world farmers;

(c) an optimal management of the progressively critical imbalance between world population trends and limited food supply; and

(d) the elimination of environmental pollution originating from conventional practices of primary waste disposal.

NOTES

1. FAO, *State of Food and Agriculture* (Rome: 1974, 1975 and 1976) 1976: pp. 3–24 and 49–78; L. R. Brown, *By Bread Alone* (New York: Praeger, 1974) chapters 14 and 15; E. Laszlo et al., *Goals for Mankind* (New York: E.P. Dutton, 1977), chapter 13; Lord Walston, *Dealing with Hunger* (London: The Bodley Head, 1976); J. Tinbergen, *Reshaping the International Order* (New York: E.P. Dutton, 1976), pp. 28–30 and chapter 11; Mesarovic and Pestel, *Mankind at the Turning Point* (New York: E.P. Dutton, 1974), chapter 9, Appendix 3; G. Borgstrom, *Harvesting the Earth* (New York: Abelard-Schuman, 1973), pp. 9–26; P. Buringh, H. van Heemst, and G. Staring, *the Absolute Maximum Food Production of the World* (Wagenigen, The Netherlands: Wagenigen Agricultural University, January 1975); M. N. Cohen, *The Food Crisis in Prehistory* (New Haven: Yale Univ. Press, 1977), pp. 18–70.

2. FAO, *Preliminary Mid-Term Review and Appraisal*, FAO/DD2/75/2 (Rome: 1975), pp. 60–62; D. Pimentel, "Energy Use in World Food Production," in *Environmental Biology* (Ithaca, N.Y.: Cornell University, 1974); President's Science Advisory Committee, *The World Food Problem* (Washington: GPO, 1967), chapter 6; UN, *Assessment of the World Feed Situation*, E/Conf/65/3 (1974), pp. 110–114; G. W. Ames, "Fetilizer Price Inflation: A Threat to the Green Revolution," *American Journal of Agricultural Economics* 57 no. 5 (1975).

3. G. Borgstrom, *Food and People Dilemma* (Mass. Duxbury Press, 1974), chapter 3; E. O. Heady et al., *World Food Production, Demand, and Trade* (Ames, Iowa: Iowa State Univ. Press, 1973), pp. 11–14; Barry Commoner, *The Poverty of Power* (New York: Alfred A. Knopf, 1976), pp. 159–175.

4. P. H. Abelson, ed., "Food," *Science* Special Compendium (1975), pp. 17–28; W. B. Jackson, "Bird and Rodent Depredation to Crops and Damage to Stored Foods—A World View," (Dayton, Ohio: Kettering Foundation, 1976); D. Pimental, "World Food Crisis: Energy and Pests," Entomological Society of America bull. 22 (1 March 1976): 20–26.

5. UN *Assessment of the World Food Situation*, p. 112.

6. Ibid. It is important to note that most of the land not now under cultivation is only marginally fertile; therefore, even if it is decided to increase the area of cultivated land to increase food supply, it will be necessary to supply greater amounts of fertilizer per unit area to the marginal land—and so the need for greater and greater quantities of fertilizer is independent of the choice we make (more area cultivated or more output per unit cultivated).

7. J. C. Meisner, "Food or Famine for the Future," *Agricultural Economics Papers*, Department of Agricultural Economics (Columbia, Missouri: University of Missouri, 1975).

FURTHER READING

Brown, L. R. *Food*. New York: Harper & Row, 1972.

Clark, C., and Haswell, M. R. *The Economics of Subsistence Agriculture*. New York: St. Martins Press, 1964.

Cook, G. J. *The Fight for Food*. London: George Harrap & Co., 1955.

Duffy, E., and Walt, A. S., eds. *The Scientific Management of Animal and Plant Communities for Conservation*. Oxford: Blackwell, 1971.

George, Susan. *How the Other Half Dies*. Montclair, N.J.: Allanheld, Osmun & Co., 1977.

Grigg, D. B. *The Agricultural System of the World*. Cambridge: Cambridge Univ. Press, 1974.

Hellman, Hal. *Feeding the World of the Future*. New York: M. Evans & Co., 1972.

FAO, *International Agricultural Adjustment*. (c75/LIM/1). Rome, 1975.

FAO, *Indicative World Plan for Agriculture.* Rome, 1970.

Hunter, Guy, A. H. Bunting, and A. Botrall. *Policy and Practice in Rural Development.* Montclair, N.J.: Allanheld, Osmun & Co., 1977.

Kellog, C. E. *Agricultural Development: Soil, Food, People, Work.* Madison, Wisconsin: Soil Science Society of America, 1975.

Lappe, Francis M. *Food First: Beyond the Myth of Scarcity.* Boston: Houghton Mifflin Co., 1977.

Makhijami, A. *Energy and Agriculture in the Third World.* Cambridge: Balinger Co., 1975.

OECD. *Unconventional Foodstuffs for Human Consumption.* Paris: OECD Headquarters, 1975.

Perelman, Michael. *Farming for Profit in a Hungry World.* Montclair, N.J.: Allanheld, Osmun & Co., 1977.

Proceedings of the Fertilizer Society: *New Developments in Manufacture and Use of Liquid Fertilizer,* 1973; *The World Food Crisis and Its Implications for the Fertilizer Industry,* 1975; *Food-Fertilizer-Energy-Efficiency,* 1975.

Rockefeller Foundation. *The Role of Animals in the World Food Situation.* New York, 1975.

University of California. *Food Task Force: A Hungry World, The Challenge to Agriculture.* Berkeley: Univ. of California Press, 1974.

University of Wagenigen. *Agricultural Science and the World Food Supply,* An International Symposium. Wagenigen, the Netherlands, 1969.

UN, *Agriculture, Science and Technology for Development,* vol. 3., New York, 1963.

Wareing, P. F., and Cooper, P. J., eds. *Potential Crop Production.* London: Heinemann Co., 1971.

WMO, *Drought and Agriculture.* Geneva; Working Group on the Assessment of Drought, 1975.

Ward, B. "A Planet to Feed," *Banker's Magazine* (of London), 1976, 1584: pp. 16–19.

PART II: THE SCOPE OF THE PROBLEM: Complexities of the Global Flow of Food, Energy and Human Waste

3

THE FOOD-ENERGY-WASTE
RELATION

The idea of waste, of something unusable, reveals an
incomplete understanding of how things work.
                                        Sim Van der Ryn*

Like other living organisms, man depends on the ecosystems
for his energy needs. Biological energy is the final good actually
consumed by man.[1] To guarantee himself adequate supplies of
energy-producing substances, man has created an incredible
number of machines, and organizational techniques of varying
complexity and efficiency.[2] As a producing organism, man
transforms air, water, and food into free energy, heat and a
residuum of unabsorbed matter. As a consuming organism, he
satisfies his biological needs by consuming energy, essentially
for growth and life-support processes. In Figures 3.1 and 3.2,
these processes—among others—are sketched as transitional
flows in the changing material states between specified input
and output points. (There will be more on these flows in
Chapters 6 and 11.) The excretion of unabsorbed matter

*The Toilet Papers (Santa Barbara, CA.: Capra Press, 1978.)

(primary human waste) is an essential part of human activity to maintain the material balance necessary to life.[3] The level of body waste in the ecosystem consists of and is maintained by the flow of unabsorbed matter that accumulates in the normal course of this process. The average man's failure to understand the part played by human body waste in the material balance in the ecosphere hardly reflects an enlightened understanding of the underlying ecological issues. In order to focus attention on them, it is useful to review some relevant facts about primary human wastes.

The ecological connection of human body waste is established by the flow of matter and energy through the natural ecosystem in accordance with the First Law of Thermodynamics: energy is indestructible.[4] (The term ecosystem refers to the complete, self-generating, marine or terrestrial natural systems of living organisms.) In natural ecosystems, two basic food

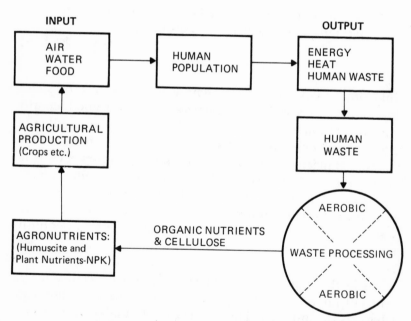

Figure 3.1 Scheme of Materials Flow in a Socio-Ecosystem via the Aerobic Process

chains exist: "the grazing food chain, consisting of the herbivores which feed on living plants together with their predators; and the detritus food chain, consisting of the herbivores which feed on dead plant materials, with their predators."[5] The grazing food chain represents certain patterns of energy linkage between different trophic categories— autotrophs, herbivores, primary carnivores, secondary carnivores—that interact in the ecological community. Detritus is an assortment of organic wastes, exudates, and dead matter that, together, constitute the primary sources of energy for the detritus food chain.

Human body waste is a major component of the total flow of matter being released by the grazing food chain to the detritus food chain. There is a large variety of organisms in the detritus community, each type dwelling in diverse areas of the soils or marine environments.[6] This food chain includes algae, bac-

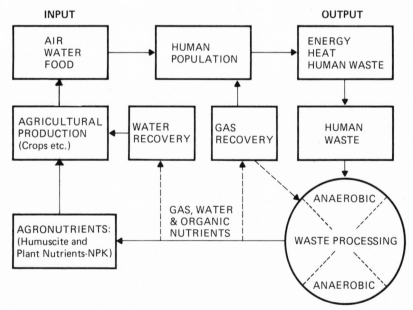

Figure 3.2 Scheme of Materials Flow in a Socio-Ecosystem via the Anaerobic Process

teria, fungi, protozoa, insects, crustacea, centipedes, worms and nematodes, to name a few. The metabolic activities of the detritus organisms are continuously integrated, vertically and horizontally, in such a way that each organism can utilize the waste products of other detritus organisms for food and energy.

THE MATERIAL DIMENSION OF BODY WASTE

Human waste is one of the three important sources of humus-forming organic residues available in the global ecosystem, the other two being plant wastes and animal wastes. The quantity of execreted human waste is determined by the efficiency of the metabolic processes, given the dietary style of the particular individual or group.[7] For human populations, the coefficient of assimilation for an average normal adult is approximately 65 percent of his material intake;[8] approximately one of every three kilograms of food and water ingested is eventually excreted as body waste. In accordance with the First Law of Thermodynamics, however, the gross outflow of metabolizable energy from one food chain is balanced by the gross inflow into another: although the amount of metabolizable energy contained in excreted matter is lost to the grazing food chain, the equivalent amount of material resources is transferred to the detritus food chain as component sources of food and energy. Of the two basic food chains—the *Grazers* and the *Decomposers*—that exist in natural ecosystems, the decomposers (the members of the detritus food chain) are of particular interest at this juncture because they represent a vital link in the process of natural absorption of human body waste. Clapham points out, in his simplified summary of the dynamics of the processes involved, that "detritus organisms ingest pieces of partially decomposed organic matter, digest them partially, and after extracting some of the chemical energy in the food to run their metabolism, excrete the remainder in the form of slightly simpler organic molecules."[9] Throughout the stages of the process, the "wastes from one organism can immediately be utilized by a second which repeat the process. . . . In most instances, the organic material has been degraded, and all that is left are some refractory organic substances termed *humic acids*, or simply humus. In a normal environment, the humus is quite stable and will form an essential part of the soil. . . ."[10] The emergence of humus does not usually terminate the long progression of biochemical degradation of organic material; only the state and the agents are altered in the continuous series of unfolding material transformations. In the succeeding phases of the formation and accumulation of humus, "a part of the elements essential for organic life, especially carbon, nitrogen, phosphorous, sulphur, and potash, become locked up and removed from circulation."[11] Because of its physical and chemical properties, humus continues to "undergo slow decomposition under certain favorable conditions." Through the process of degradation, it "tends to supply a slow but continuous stream of the elements necessary for new plant synthesis."[12] Lastly, one cannot overlook the strategic function of humus in soil formation. Through its sustaining influence on the soil, humus serves as a regulator of plant growth in terrestrial environments, as well "as a reserve and a stabilizer for organic life on this planet."[13]

These points may be summarized briefly. The ecological route of body waste can be traced from the grazing food chain through a long chain of metabolic degradations into humic acids or humus, and through the formation of soils, a source of nutrients for plants and other organisms, back to the grazing food chain. This model of a natural ecosystem is a simplified analytical description of a complex dynamic process illustrating the cyclical flow of matter and energy through biotic and abiotic environments, their general interaction, and the interdependence of organisms present at different trophic levels.[14] In the present case, such a model is helpful in promoting a general understanding of the underlying processes in a functional state.

The role of man in maintaining the natural balance is crucial. There are a number of ways in which the cumulative effect of man's activity may stabilize or upset the balance of the ecosystem. The flow and absorption of human body waste into our global ecosystem, discussed in the next section, is an important example. In this connection, it is important to realize that nations:

> have been making technological choices that have been displacing products and processes which fit in with the cycles of nature. Then to rescue nature, we have been applying "environmental technology" which substitutes for natural processes, and therefore duplicates the work available from the ecological sector. This displacement and duplication is a crippling economic handicap. Consider the example of how we handle human waste. As the growth of urban areas has become more and more concentrated, much energy, including research and development work, has gone into developing and implementing technologies to protect our lakes and rivers and coastal waters from the wastes we are dumping into them. These wastes, however, are themselves rich sources of chemical energy capable of being recycled back to the farmlands from which these nutrients came. They would replace much of the fertilizer that we produce from fossil fuels and eliminate the need for energy—expensive tertiary sewage treatment.[15]

NOTES

1. Although man eats vast quantities of plant and animal substances as an omnivorous organism, he only consumes energy. In other words, man does not directly consume what he eats. See Nicholas Georgescu-Roegen, *The Entropy Law and the Economic Process* (Cambridge: Harvard University Press, 1971), pp. 277–78; D. Le Vay, *Human Anatomy and Physiology* (London: English University Press, 1974), pp. 33–37; Lewis Mumford, *Technics and Civilization* (New York: Harcourt Brace & Co.), pp. 373–380; J. Phillipson, *Ecological Energetics* (New York: St. Martins Press, 1966), chapter 1.

2. W. H. G. Armytage, *The Rise of the Technocrats* (Toronto: University of Toronto Press, 1965), pp. 92–93; UN, *Science and Technology for Development*, vol. 1 (New York, 1963), chapter 1; Norbert Wiener, *Cybernet-*

ics (New York: John Wiley & Sons, 1948); Barry Commoner, *The Poverty of Power* (New York: Alfred A. Knopf, 1976), pp. 19–32.

3. P. Handler, ed., *Biology and the Future of Man* (New York: University Press, 1970), pp. 88–93; D. Le Vay, op. cit.; F. W. Sunderman and F. Boerner "Feces," in *Normal Values in Clinical Medicine* (Philadelphia: W. B. Saunders, 1950), pp. 254–261.

4. G. Hatsopoulos and J. Keenan, *Principles of General Thermodynamics* (New York: John Wiley & Sons, 1965), pp. 22–35; Barry Commoner, op. cit., p. 5; *Encyclopedia Brittanica: Micropaedia*, vol. 9, p. 947.

5. E. P. Odum, *Fundamentals of Ecology* 3rd ed. (Philadelphia: W. B. Saunders, 1971), p. 63; J. Phillipson, op. cit., pp. 6–7.

6. E. P. Odum, op. cit., pp. 9–10.

7. Ibid., pp. 75–79; J. Phillipson, op. cit., pp. 6–7.

8. Estimated from data on human metabolic turnover. For definitions and raw data, see J. W. B. Clapham, *Natural Ecosystem* (New York: Macmillan, 1973), pp. 25, 28, 31; J. Phillipson, op. cit., pp. 6–7; E. P. Odum, op. cit., pp. 67, 76; J. McHale, *World Facts and Trends* (New York: Collier Books, 1972), pp. 32–33; D. P. Burkitt, "Epidemiology of Cancer of the Colon and Rectum," *Cancer* (July 1971), pp. 3–11; D. P. Burkitt, "Effect of Dietary Fibre on Stools and Transit Times and Its Role in the Causation of Disease," *The Lancet* (20 December 1972): 1408–1412; J. B. Lawes, *The Sewage of London* (London: W. Trounce, Printer, 1855), pp. 4–34; A. C. Rendtorf and M. Kashagarian, "Stool Patterns of Healthy Adult Males," *Journal of American Protologic Society* (May–June 1967): pp. 222–228; P. J. Cammidge, *The Feces of Children and Adults* (New York: W. Wood & Co., 1914), pp. 6–7; M. A. Eastwood, J. R. Kirkpatrick, W. D. Mitchell, Ann Bone, and T. Hamilton, "Effects of Dietary Supplements of Wheat, Bran and Cellulose on Feces and Bowel Function," *British Medical Journal* (17 November 1973): pp. 392–394; Sunderman and Boerner, op. cit., pp. 254–261.

9. W. B. Clapham, Jr., op. cit. p. 33. For a more formal discussion of the processes involved, see E. P. Odum, op. cit., pp. 63–68.

10. J. W. Clapham, op. cit.; also W. Flaig, "An Introductory Review of Humic Substances . . .," *Humic Substances*, Proc. of International Mtg. on Humic Substances (Nieuwersluis, Pudoc, Wageningen, 1972), pp. 19–42; M. M. Kononova, *Soil Organic Matter*, 2nd ed. (New York: Pergamon Press, 1966), pp. 13–45.

11. S. A. Waksman, *Humus* (Baltimore: M. Wilkins Co., 1938), p. xii.

12. S. A. Waksman, op. cit.; also M. M. Kononova, op. cit.

13. S. A. Waksman, op. cit.

14. For a more comprehensive discussion of the subject, the reader is referred to E. P. Odum, op. cit., p. 555.

15. Mark Hatfield, in *Energy: Today's Choices, Tomorrow's Opportunities*, A. B. Schmalz, ed. (Washington, D.C.: World Future Society, 1974).

FURTHER READING

Borgstrom, G. "Food, Feed & Energy." *Ambio,* vol. II no. 6, 1973.

Blaxter, K. "Power and Agricultural Revolution." *New Scientist,* 14 February 1974.

Buringh, van Heemst & Staring. *The Absolute Maximum Food Production of the World.* Wagenigen, The Netherlands: Wagenigen Agricultural University, January, 1975.

Cooke, J. W. *Fertilizing for Maximum Yield.* London: Crosby Lockwood & Co., 1972.

Hulme, A. C. *Biochemistry of Fruits and Their Products.* New York: Academic Press, 1971. Vols. I and II.

Jones, J. G. W., ed. *The Biological Efficiency of Protein Production.* Cambridge: Cambridge University Press, 1973.

Kramer, A. *Food and the Consumer.* AVI Publications, 1973.

Krutilla, J. V., and Fisher, A. C. *The Economics of Natural Environments.* Baltimore: Johns Hopkins Press, 1975.

Lawrie, R. A., ed. *Proteins as Human Food.* Butterworth Co., 1970.

Rappaport, A. R. "The Flow of Energy in an Agricultural Society." *American Scientist,* February 1974.

Romberger, J. A., ed., *Biosystematics in Agriculture,* Proceedings of the Second Annual Symposium in Agricultural Research, Beltsville Agricultural Research Center. Montclair, N.J.: Allanheld, Osmun & Co., 1978

Russell, S. E. J. *Fertilizers in Modern Agriculture.* 3rd ed. HMSO, 1939.

Schuffelen, A. C. "Energy Balance in the Use of Fertilizers." *Span,* vol. 18, no. 1, 1975.

Schuphen, W. *Nutritional Values in Crops and Plants,* Problems for Producers and Consumers. Faber & Faber, 1965.

von Monsjou, I. W. "Food-Fertilizer-Energy-Efficiency." *Proceedings of the Fertilizer Society* no. 152. London, 1975.

4

POPULATION AND THE GLOBAL VOLUME OF HUMAN WASTE

The human waste of a million people spread over an
extensive rural area, does not in terms of pollution
constitute the same load on the water recipients and
their cleansing capabilities in the same way as when
concentrated and coming from a city of a million.

G. Borgstrom*

Man's life-support activity is an input-output process that
depends on the intake of oxygen and food and the generation of
energy through the metabolic processes. The waste products of
this activity consist mainly of water, carbon dioxide, and
certain nitrogenous breakdowns of proteins such as urea.[1] The
exact composition of body waste will vary with the kind of
food, fluid intake, and genetic factors. In general, the solid and
liquid wastes excreted by the bowels are derived mainly from
substances formed within the intestines, and they consist
mostly of water plus some mineral salts, such as calcium
phosphate, and a considerable quantity of nitrogenous material, mainly from dead bacteria.[2] The kidneys are responsible for

*"Food and Ecology," in *Ecosphere*, vol. 2 no. 1 (1971), p. 11.

the removal of waste products and excess water from the blood, mainly in the form of urine. The material constituents of urine are derived from ingested food and fluids, and partly from the oxidative processes of tissues, as are the organic and inorganic contents such as urea, uric acid, phosphates, and sulfates.[3]

THE FLOW AND COMPOSITION OF BODY WASTE

The term body waste, as used in this discussion, refers only to human biological wastes, especially feces and urine output. Body waste flow rate varies widely, and the form, consistency, and composition are determined largely by genetic, biological, and cultural (i.e. dietary) factors.[4] Among the authoritative studies in this area, Burkitt's investigations[5] correlating intestinal transit rates and form of the stool indicate an initial appearance time with mean values ranging from 12.8 hours for a population of school students living on unrefined diet in rural South Africa to 45.7 hours for a population of white naval ratings living on refined diet in the United Kingdom. Full transit time averaged 33.5 hours for the former to 83.4 hours for the latter. Genetic and cultural factors such as the capacity to digest and absorb lactic substances, also influence intestinal transit rates, as do the dietary habits of vegetarians.[6] In general, the amount of fecal matter excreted by the average normal adult varies between 100 to 200 grams within a 24-hour time unit.[7] The water content for the normal adult is estimated between 65 and 70 percent and the dry matter approximately 30 to 35 percent, of the bulk.[8] In chemical analysis, the constituents of a typical sample of the feces of a normal adult include nitrogen, potassium, phosphorous, sodium, chloride, ammonia, calcium, and sulphur, and other minerals.

SOME IMPLICATIONS OF BODY WASTE OUTPUT

It is obvious that the global output of body waste increases with population growth. To underline the magnitudes involved, a graphical summary of the prevailing global trends of population growth and the outflow of body waste is presented in Figure 4.1. Bumper crops of people are yielding millions who cannot be fed or cared for adequately.[9] The human population, which currently increases by at least one million people per year, has unfortunately become a demographic time bomb on this planet,[10] and by the year 2000, the world population may range between seven and eight billion. Certain functional questions arise in connection with such potentially explosive development. Will the known resources of the earth, however well managed, be adequate to feed, house, and educate such a magnitude of people? Is the world community aware of the impending pollution crisis and of the major contributions which the body waste of seven or eight billion people will make to the ever increasing level of aquacidal and terracidal pollutants? Two basic problems are associated with the world food supply, and both are linked to the physiological nature of man. The primary problem, which so far has received the greatest attention, arises from the technical or production side, namely the "supply factor"; the second, the derivative biological problem arises from the relation between food consumption and the inherent constraint imposed by the assimilation factor.

The derivative problem of food consumption arises from the fact that human assimilation is estimated to be 0.65, as indicated in Chapter 3, which implies that about one-third of man's food and water intake is eventually excreted as metabolic waste. For purposes of quantitative description, Table 4.1 presents global estimates of the flow of metabolic waste for the postwar period.[11] The annual figures for each year are the sums of the combined quantities of body waste separately estimated for the populations of developed and developing areas. On the average, the proportion of global figures originating in the underdeveloped areas is about seventy percent of the total. In 1950, when the world population was about 2.5 billion, the global output of body waste was estimated at about one billion metric tons. The average quantity per day for the same year was equivalent to about 3.2 million metric tons. By 1975, with a

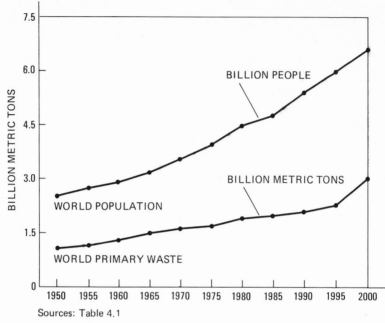

Sources: Table 4.1

Figure 4.1 Estimates of World Population and Levels of Human Waste

world population estimated at about 4.2 billion, the global output of body waste had risen to nearly 2 billion metric tons. During the 25 years between 1950 and 1975, the estimated global output of body waste per capita/per year was approximately half a million metric tons. The global output per day had risen to about 5.2 million metric tons in the meantime. The latter figure was 2 million metric tons greater than the corresponding level of output in 1950, and the trend continues. In another 25 years, around 2000 A.D., the projected global levels of body waste per day will be 8.5 million metric tons, or 3 million metric tons higher than the level for 1950. If present trends continue, the projected annual level of output for the year 2000 is at least 3 billion metric tons.

TABLE 4.1. Estimates of Population and Levels of Human Waste: Global Figures.

	1950	1955	1960	1965	1970	1975	1980	1985	1990	1995	2000
Population figures (millions)	2486	2713	2982	3289	3732	4201	4517	4876	5383	5943	6661
					million metric tons						
Annual output of human waste	1177	1285	1413	1558	1769	1989	2141	2310	2550	2816	3156
Annual output developing countries	832	908	998	1100	1263	1386	1526	1631	1801	1988	2243
Annual output – developed countries	346	378	415	458	506	603	615	679	749	827	913
Daily global output	3.2	3.5	3.8	4.2	4.7	5.3	5.7	6.2	6.8	7.5	8.5

Principal sources: See detailed references in Appendix A.

NOTES

1. D. Le Vay, *Human Anatomy and Physiology* (London: English University Press, 1974), pp. 43, 315 and 402.

2. P. J. Cammidge, *The Feces of Children and Adults* (New York: W. Wood & Co., 1914), pp. 6–10; D. Le Vay, op. cit., p. 315; F. W. Sunderman and F. Boerner, "Feces," in *Normal Values in Clinical Medicine* (Philadelphia: W. B. Saunders & Co., 1950).

3. D. Le Vay, op. cit., pp. 403–404; Sunderman and Boerner, op. cit.

4. P. Handler, *Biology and the Future of Man* (New York: Oxford University Press, 1970), pp. 255–256; D. P. Burkitt, "Epidemiology of Cancer of the Colon and Rectum," *Cancer* (July 1971); R. C. Rendtorf and M. Kashagarian, "Stool Patterns of Adult Males," *Journal of American Protological Society* (May–June 1967).

5. D. P. Burkitt, "Effect of Dietary Fibre on Stools and Transit Times and Its Role in the Causation of Disease," *The Lancet* (20 December 1972). Also refs. 2, 3 and 4 above.

6. The vegetable eaters normally excrete large, thick, soft feces, whereas the meat eaters excrete small, dried and "often scybalous" feces. See Cammidge, op. cit., pp. 7, 15, 202; Sunderman and Boerner, op. cit., pp. 254–261.

7. In special cases, such as fasting and pathological cholera, men have been found to excrete as little as 7 to 8 gm and as much as 500–1200 gm of feces respectively in 24-hour periods. See Cammidge, op. cit., p. 6.

8. *Todd-Sanford Clinical Diagnosis*, 14th ed. (Philadelphia: W. B. Saunders & Co., 1969), p. 781.

9. J. D. Tydings, *Born to Starve* (New York: William Morrow & Co., 1970), pp. 3–94.

10. Ibid., p. 3ff.

11. See Table 4.1 and Figure 4.1. Estimated from global population and human metabolic output data. See UN, *Demographic Yearbook* 1975; J. B. Lawes, *The Sewage of London* (London: W. Trounce, Printer, 1855); P. J. Cammidge, op. cit., pp. 607; Rendtorf and Kashagarian, op. cit., pp. 6–7; D. P. Burkitt, 1971 and 1972, op. cit.; M. A. Eastwood, "Effects of Dietary Supplements of Wheat, Bran and Cellulose on Feces and Bowel Function," *British Medical Journal* (17 November 1973); Sunderman and Boerner, op. cit.; A. C. Garg et al., *Organic Manure* (New Delhi: Indian Council of Agricultural Research, 1971); J. McHale, *World Facts and Trends* (New York: Collier Books, 1972); P. L. Jaiswal, *Handbook of Manures and Fertilizers* (New Delhi: ICAR, 1971).

FURTHER READING

Brady, N. D., ed. *Agriculture and Quality of our Environment*. Washington: Soil Science Society of America, 1967.

Devik, O. *Harvesting Polluted Waters*. New York: Plenum Press, 1976.

Department of the Environment. *Pollution: Nuisance or Nemesis?*, London: HMSO, 1972.

Gainey, P. C. *Microbiology of Water and Sewage*. New York: Prentice-Hall, 1952.

Gloyna, E. *Waste Stabilization Ponds*. Geneva: WHO, 1971.

Hawkes, H. A. *The Ecology of Waste Water Treatment*. New York: Pergamon Press, 1963.

Marx, L. *Waste*. New York: Harper & Row, 1971.

McGauhey, P. *Earth's Tolerance for Wastes*. Texas Quarterly 2, 1968.

Mellamby, Sir Kenneth. *The Threat of World Pollution*. London: Lindsey Press, 1971.

UK, Cabinet Office. *Future World Trends . . .*, in Population, Resources and Pollution, etc. London: HMSO, 1976.

Wagner, E. G. *Excreta Disposal for Rural Areas and Small Communities*. Geneva: WHO, 1958.

Walker, C. *Environmental Pollution by Chemicals*. London: Hutchinson Co., 1971.

WHO. *Problems in Community Wastes Management*. Public Health Papers, no. 38. Geneva, 1969.

5

ECOLOGICAL DIMENSIONS OF HUMAN WASTE: ORGANIC HUMUS AND PLANT NUTRIENTS

> . . . the Almighty has endowed the same particles of matter with the property of entering into a variety of forms, at one time the most offensive, and at another the most attractive. In this ever changing circle nothing is without its value, nothing is lost.
>
> J. B. Lawes*

There are two coexisting grand designs in the ecosphere: the Grand Design of Nature (GDN) and the Grand Design of Man (GDM). In the GDN, everything works out according to natural laws;[1] but in the GDM, everything does not work out according to man's design.[2] Because of the underlying differences between them, the two processes tend to produce qualitatively contrasting systems. The GDM has evolved certain types of communities with deleterious side effects that include wastes, contaminants, and pollutants. Analogously, the GDN tends to evolve dynamically balanced ecological

*The Sewage of London (London: W. Trounce, Printer, 1855), p. 4.

communities plus certain undesirable side effects that include few, if any, wastes, contaminants, or pollutants. In socio-ecosystems, environmental pollutants tend to result from excessive or concentrated contamination of the local ecology by improper human response to man-made wastes.[3] It is an empirical fact that, in urban environments, policies that promote nonintegrated methods of collection and disposal of human body waste will inevitably create environmental pollution. Conversely, policies which promote maximum recovery and utilization of body waste tend to augment the amount of energy available for social utilization and also aid in minimizing, if not eliminating, environmental pollution.[4]

If the postwar levels of global output of human waste were dumped on the surface of the globe, the average level of concentration per square mile would be as follows: 6.0 metric tons in 1950; 7.2 metric tons in 1960; 8.7 metric tons in 1970; and 9.6 metric tons in 1975. If the levels of concentrations were computed exclusively on the basis of earth's land area, the corresponding figures (per square mile) would be significantly higher: *for earth's land area*: 20.5 metric tons in 1950; 24.6 metric tons in 1960; 29.9 metric tons in 1970; and 33.0 metric tons in 1975. The relevant figures based on *earth's water area* are: 8.4 metric tons in 1950; 10.1 metric tons in 1960; 12.3 metric tons in 1970; and 13.6 metric tons in 1975. If the average concentration of body waste is restricted to the amount of the *earth's arable land*, the corresponding figures per square mile are as follows: 196.9 metric tons in 1950; 232.0 metric tons in 1960; 284.9 metric tons in 1970; and 314.4 metric tons in 1975. (See Table 5.1.)[5]

The social and ecological consequences of improper body waste disposal are potentially dangerous to life particularly in crowded urban communities; the toxic effects are inescapable even in sparsely populated villages and rural areas.[6] For mankind, the ultimate social environment and geophysical frame of reference is the whole earth. Within that space, the ecological consequences of improper disposal of human body waste are, in the long and short run, unfavorable to the well-being and survival of man.

TABLE 5.1. Estimates of Agronutrients Recoverable from Human Waste: Global Figures (in million metric tons).

	1950	1955	1960	1965	1970	1975	1980	1985	1990	1995	2000
Recoverable humuscite (Ω)	60.0	65.0	70.0	80.0	90.0	99.0	110.0	115.0	125.0	140.0	155.0
Recoverable nitrogen (N)	10.8	11.7	13.0	14.3	16.0	18.2	19.5	21.2	23.4	25.6	29.0
Recoverable phosphorous (P)	4.2	4.6	5.1	5.6	6.3	7.1	7.6	8.3	9.1	10.0	11.4
Recoverable potassium (K)	2.6	2.8	3.1	3.5	3.9	4.4	4.7	5.1	5.7	6.2	7.0
Total Recoverable (N,P,K)	17.70	19.10	21.24	23.40	26.20	29.70	31.90	34.70	38.20	41.80	47.40

Principal sources: See detailed references in Appendix A.

The modern history of social response to problems caused by the rising concentration of body waste and its local disposal began in the late eighteenth century. Judging from the published accounts of the Royal Commission in England in the first decade of the nineteenth century and from subsequent investigations by other private and official bodies in Europe and elsewhere, the response seems to have reflected a crisis-oriented, single-minded preoccupation with social sanitation and public health. However effective the pioneering measures in social sanitation were, the main approaches to the problems inevitably promoted an essentially one-dimensional solution, in almost total isolation from other vital aspects of the body waste problems. Commenting in 1863, J. B. Lawes pointed out that the "question of the sanitary arrangements of our towns was taken up by engineers before agricultural chemistry was much studied, and they have committed us to plans which, though they effectively remove the noxious matter from our dwellings, . . . at the same time, have tended greatly to the pollution of our streams."[7]

The sewage system as we know it has been rendered anachronistic by the needs of today's world. At best a mechanical albatross, modern sewage is, at worst, a source of endless pollution. Professor Wolman, in 1956, wrote that the world community is "still badly in need of a treatment process which is cheaper than any so far developed for water-carried waste. Secondly, the disposal of sludge resulting from such water-carried waste is still unsatisfactory."[8] More than 100 years ago, J. B. Lawes raised the same questions before the Chemical Society of London. He declared that it was "no less true than strange that, after so many centuries of advance in regard to almost every other requirement of civilized life, the lesson should not yet have been learnt of how to dispose of the excretal matter of large populations, in such a manner as to secure both their collection, removal . . . and . . . economic utilization. . . ."[9]

A century ago, the limited-objective, one-dimensional solution to the problems of human body wastes was acceptable. In today's world, some 4.5 billion people produce excretal matters at about 5.5 million metric tons every 24 hours, close to 2 billion metric tons per year. Man now occupies a time/growth dimension in which the world population doubles in 35 years or less. In this new universe, there is only one viable and ecologically consistent solution to the body waste problems— the processing and application of primary waste for its agronutrient content.

Students of soil science maintain that humus does not provide plant foods directly. Most of them agree, however, that it is a vital source of essential plant nutrients that include carbon, nitrogen, phosphorous, and sulfur liberated by the activities of microorganisms.[10] A wide variety of physical and biochemical reactions between humus and the inorganic constituents of soils are energized by adequate supplies of humus. Organic humus can provide those major elements— nitrogen, phosphate, potassium (N-P-K)—supplied by modern agricultural fertilizers, under favorable conditions.[11] As indicated in earlier chapters, there are three major sources of humus-forming organic residues in the ecosystem: plant wastes, animal wastes, and human wastes. Throughout agricultural history, different combinations of nutrients from these sources have been utilized to maintain soil fertility.[12] This chapter elaborates on the function of human body waste in producing humus.

Humus may be defined as a natural body of organic matter ranging in color from brown to black,[13] and broadly classified "according to the degree of its incorporation into the mineral soil, the types of organisms involved in its decomposition, and the vegetation from which it is derived."[14] Based on general chemical analysis, the composition of humus is about 60 percent carbon, 6 percent nitrogen, and smaller quantities of phosphorous, sulfur, and other ingredients. The microbial and biochemical origins of humus have been subjects of active investigations for several hundred years, leading progressively to present global research that seeks expanded technical knowledge about different phases or organic life in soils.

Today, organic humus is in demand in many areas of industrial activity. In the fields of agriculture and horticulture, humus is valuable because its renewable stores of vital ingredients economically provide nutrients essential for plant growth, increase water absorption by soil, and improve soil workability. Finally, in addition to its permanent role in the formation of most soils, the global layer of humus naturally "serves as a reserve and a stabilizer for organic life on this planet."[15]

The humus content of soil is constantly being used up.[16] This is one of the factors governing the dynamic changes in soil fertility. In the total context of the living soil, the three properties of humus relevant to soil fertility are the physical, the biological, and the chemical. Among the physical influences, the presence of humus helps bind together a light and crumbly soil and is effective in rendering a heavy soil more friable. It provides better aeration, increases heat and absorption capacity, and augments the buffering properties of soils. The biological properties of humus are vital to the natural maintenance of soil fertility. By favoring growth of common saprophytic soil bacteria, fungi, protozoa and nematodes, organic humus promotes the growth and activities of the soil organisms whose work is indispensable in maintaining the soil's natural fecundity. Chemically, organic humus represents a rich storehouse of elements needed for plant growth. The metabolic activities of microorganisms and the resulting decomposition of organic matter liberate a complex stream of gases and salts that include carbon dioxide, nitrogen-ammonia, phosphorous and other plant foods.[17]

Under normal cropping, soil needs an abundant supply of humus to maintain its fertility, just as the crops need abundant fertilizers to grow and mature properly. To insure an adequate supply of humus, built-in self-regulating mechanisms are at work in the natural ecosystem and, to some extent, in the socio-ecosystem as well. The natural process whereby deficiencies in soil fertility and plant nutrients are eventually corrected operates in a manner consistent with the general equilibrium dynamics of the ecosystem. There are essential differences, however, between the natural ecosystem (e.g., a forest estate or wilderness) and the socio-ecosystem (e.g., an agricultural estate or a farming community) both in their structural properties and in the mutability of their self-regulating mechanisms. In particular, the optimal limits of cropping are not analogous for soils in both categories. This condition may be explained, in part, by the behavior of a human population which must nevertheless take long-term measures to prevent the onset of desertification and concomitant soil disturbance resulting from over-cropping and over-grazing. The question arising is not whether, but how best to maintain adequate levels of soil fertility, and how best to supply the plant nutrients required for optimum cropping of its soils (i.e., the level of output consistent with population growth policy). Above all, it is important to remember that in meeting the biochemical and physical needs of soils and plants, organic humus and fertilizers play essentially complementary, not competitive, roles. To provide the elements of soil fertility, organic humus plays a direct role, while the role of fertilizers is indirect. Corresondingly, in providing the plant-food element, fertili-ers play a direct role, while organic humus plays an indirect role. In socio-ecosystems, therefore, the availability of humus is vital to insure optimum soil fertility, just as the application of fertilizers is crucial to insure optimum cropping. Since organic humus and fertilizers are not perfect complements in agri-cultural and horticultural production functions, there are certain possibilities of technical substitutions between them,[18] however limited in range.

Modern fertilizers are synthetically produced from chemicals and supplied in varying concentrations and combinations of nitrates, phosphates, and potassium (N-P-K) to suit different nutrient needs of soil. But the humus content of soils under permanent cultivation can be provided only in a limited number of ways, such as by digging or ploughing in animal and sewage manures, by composting all organic wastes, or by growing green manure crops.

The ecological function of organic humus enhances the natural fertility of soils. As an integral part of the overall geo-bio-chemical processes, the evolutionary process involved in the making of organic humus is active under favorable circumstances. Undoubtedly, the resource-creating aspects of the dynamic processes are of historical as well as practical interest to man. This continuing process of "creative destruction" (the creation, accumulation, and degradation of humus) predates the appearance of man and the evolution of farming by billions of years. Unlike many other planetary resources, organic humus is truly a "renewable" capital endowment whose global value and significance in agriculture and ecodevelopment are yet to be fully appreciated.

For many thousands of years, farmers recognized the value of and treasured the nutrients in body waste and animal and green manures, as the main sources of plant foods.[19] With the introduction of mineral fertilizers more than 100 years ago, the production, utilization and the availability of plant nutrients have affected fundamental changes in the course of world agricultural development. By 1975, the use of organic manures was vanishing rapidly, except in some developing countries where such practices are still in their final stages of decline. It is ironic to note that as the application of mineral fertilizers became accepted worldwide, the human and animal races that are the major source of organic manures have increased so rapidly that their respective populations are now doubling at shorter and shorter time intervals. The potential economic and ecological benefits to be realized from an optimal body waste management program are great. From the economic perspective, the recovery of agronutrients—humuscite, nitrogen, phosphorous, potassium—from body waste is a technological and, hopefully, an economical reality. And the potential for ecological gains from transforming environmental pollutants into agronutrients is demonstrably high.[20] As will be shown in Chapters 6 and 11, in both ancient and modern times, farmers have been well aware that humus material made under appropriate conditions and with varying concentrations of body waste could be used safely for farming and other agricultural activities.[21] Recent technical advances also confirm that plant nutrients and humus can be recovered from body waste and safely restored to the soil, not only to provide long-lasting organic manures, but also to prevent the decline in soil fertility caused by continuous agricultural cropping.[22]

It is useful to examine here, through Tables 5.1, 5.3 and 5.4, the potentials for recovery of agronutrients from body waste in today's world. In 1950, for example, the total amount of potentially recoverable agronutrients from body waste alone was conservatively estimated at about 60 million metric tons of humuscite, with a complement of at least 17 million metric tons of N-P-K nutrients.[23] Humuscite is a bulky biologically based soil nutrient consisting of stabilized organic residue from processed body waste. In comparative terms, the magnitude of recoverable agronutrients was at least four times the equivalent of global production and consumption figures combined for all chemical fertilizers in 1950.[24]

Although the global postwar consumption for chemical fertilizers rose quite rapidly—and was doubling every 10 years from 1950—the potential amounts of recoverable agronutrients corresponding to each year between 1950 and 1975 increased faster than the rate indicated for chemical fertilizers. According to FAO sources, global consumption figures of combined chemical fertilizers for selected years are: 13.8 million metric tons in 1950; 29.6 million metric tons in 1960; 68.3 million metric tons in 1970; and about 92.9 million metric tons in 1975. These and other related figures on consumption, plus a set of relevant figures on global production of chemical fertilizers are presented in Tables 5.3 and 5.4. The corresponding figures for recoverable agronutrients are: 1950, 60 million metric tons of humuscite, and about 17 million metric tons of N-P-K nutrients; 1960, 70 million metric tons of humuscite, and about 21 million metric tons of N-P-K nutrients; 1970, 90 million metric tons of humuscite, and about 26 million metric tons of N-P-K nutrients; and in 1975, 100 million metric tons of humuscite, and about 29 million metric tons of N-P-K

TABLE 5.2. Estimated Money Value of Agronutrients Recoverable from Human Waste: Global Figures (at 1975 world f.o.b. prices) (in billion dollars).

	1950	1955	1960	1965	1970	1975	1980	1985	1990	1995	2000
Total value of recoverable N, P, and K	6.93	7.53	8.36	9.21	10.31	11.56	12.53	13.63	15.03	16.46	18.67
Recoverable nitrogen	4.78	5.19	5.76	6.34	7.09	7.97	8.64	9.40	10.37	11.35	12.86
Recoverable phosphorous	1.82	1.99	2.20	2.42	2.72	3.04	3.29	3.59	3.93	4.32	4.93
Recoverable potassium	0.33	0.36	0.39	0.44	0.50	0.55	0.60	0.65	0.73	0.79	0.89

Principal sources: See detailed references in Appendix A.

TABLE 5.3. Fertilizer Consumption: Global Figures (in million metric tons).

	1950	1955	1960	1965	1970	1975	1980[a]
Nitrogen fertilizer (N)	3.9	6.6	10.0	17.5	31.2	46.5	60.6
Phosphorous fertilizer (P)	5.7	7.8	9.9	14.4	19.8	26.2	31.1
Potassium fertilizer (K)	4.1	6.8	8.5	12.2	16.5	23.0	29.5
Aggregate consumption (N,P,K)	13.8	21.2	28.5	44.0	68.3	95.7	121.2

[a]Projection: See Appendix A for principal sources.

TABLE 5.4. Fertilizer Production: Global Figures (in million metric tons).

	1950	1955	1960	1965	1970	1975	1980[a]
Nitrogen fertilizer (N)	4.0	7.2	10.6	19.2	32.9	47.0	62.0
Phosphorous fertilizer (P)	5.7	8.0	10.0	15.1	20.8	31.0	33.5
Potassium fertilizer (K)	4.5	7.1	8.7	13.8	17.9	32.0	32.1
Aggregate production (N,P,K)	14.3	22.3	29.3	48.0	71.6	110.0	127.6

[a]Projection of data from principal sources: See Appendix A.
Principal sources: See Appendix A.

nutrients.[25] The global figures have been disaggregated[26] in order to obtain additional information on the composition of recoverable agronutrients. It may be inferred from these figures that tens of millions of metric tons of agronutrients—with substantial amounts of organic humus and plant foods—could have been recovered and utilized as natural supplements to commercial fertilizers in the last 25 years. If present trends in population, food, and fiber consumption continue, potential levels of recoverable agronutrients from human body waste alone could rise to more than 100 million metric tons in 1980, 127 million metric tons in 1990, and more than 200 million metric tons in the first decade of the twenty-first century.

NOTES

1. Lamont Cole, "The Ecosphere," *Scientific American* (April 1958): 83–92; E. P. Odum, *Ecology* (Athens, Ga.: University of Georgia Press, 1963), p. 1053; E. P. Odum, *Fundamentals of Ecology* 3rd ed. (Philadelphia: W. B. Saunders & Co., 1971), pp. 8–36.

2. S. Brubaker, *To Live on Earth* (Baltimore: Johns Hopkins University Press, 1972), chapter 2; Barry Commoner, "On the Meaning of Ecological Failures in International Development," in *The Careless Technology*, M. T. Farvar, ed. (New York: Natural History Press, 1971), pp. xxi–xxix; R. F. Dasman, J. P. Milton, and P. H. Freeman, *Ecological Principles for Economic Development* (New York: John Wiley & Sons, 1973), pp. 15–50.

3. S. Brubaker, op. cit., pp. 49–57.

4. A. C. Garg et al., *Organic Manure* (New Delhi: Indian Council of Agricultural Research, 1971), pp. 1–148; FAO, *Organic Material as Fertilizers*, Soils Bulletin 27 (Rome 1975), pp. 19–30; L. A. Stevens, "The County that Reclaims its Sewage," *Reader's Digest* (July 1975): 39–44; FAO, *Organic Materials and Soil Productivity*, Soils Bulletin 35 (Rome, 1977).

5. Estimated from figures in Table 4 and supplementary data from Hamond Medallion *World Atlas* (New Jersey, 1971), pp. 1–3; *National Geographic Atlas of the World*, 4th ed. (Washington, D.C.: 1975), National Geographic Society, 1975, pp. 7–8.

6. A. Welman, "Disposal of Man's Wastes," in *Man's Role in Changing the Face of the Earth*, W. L. Thomes, ed., (Chicago: University of Chicago Press, 1956), vol. 2, pp. 807–816.

7. J. B. Lawes, "Utilization of Town Sewage," *Journal of Royal Agricultural Society of England*, vol. 24 (1863): 26.

8. A. Welman, op. cit., p. 810.

9. J. B. Lawes, "Composition, Value and Utilization of Town Sewage," *Journal of the Chemical Society* (March–April 1866): 2.

10. FAO, *Organic Materials and Soil Productivity*, op. cit.; W. A. J. Flaig, "An Introductory Review of Humic Substances," op. cit., pp. 19–42; S. L. Janssen, "Role of Humus Formation and Decomposition in the Terrestrial Nitrogen Cycles," in *Humic Substances*, Proc. of International Mtg. on Humic Substances (Nieuwersluis, Pudoc, Wageningen, 1972) pp. 123–135; M. M. Kononova, *Soil Organic Matter*, 2nd ed., (New York: Pergamon Press, 1966), pp. 13–45; F. Lemaine, "Influences of Organic Matter on the Phosphate Nutrition of Plants," *Studies About Humus* symposium, Prague, 1967, pp. 302–305; W. Rawald, "On the Possibility of Characterizing the Influence of Humic Substances on the Nitrification and Uptake of Nitrates by Plants" in *Studies about Humus*, op. cit., pp. 293–296; S. A. Waksman, *Humus* (Baltimore: M. Wilkins Co., 1938), p. xii.

11. FAO, *Organic Materials as Fertilizers*, op. cit., pp. 19–71; A. C. Garg, op. cit., pp. 2–14; D. P. Hopkins, *Chemicals, Humus and the Soil* (New York: Chemical Publishing Co., 1948) pp. 11–132; J. J. C. Van Voorhoeve, "Organic Fertilizers: Problems and Potentials for Developing Countries" in IBRD Fertilizer Study (Washington, D.C.: IBRD, 1974); FAO, *Organic Materials and Soil Productivity*, op. cit.

12. A. H. Bunting, "Experiments on Organic Manures 1942–49," *Journal of Agricultural Science* 60 (1949): 121–140; A. Duncan, "Economic Aspects of the Use of Organic Materials as Fertilizers," in FAO, *Organic Materials as Fertilizers*, pp. 352–378; H. Gottas, *Composting*, WHO Monograph 31 (Geneva, 1956); E. Mather and F. J. Hart, "The Geography of Manure," *Compost Science* (winter 1969), pp. 27–32; *The Bible*, Daniel, 2:5 and 3:20; Mamuni Parasara, *Krishi Sangraha*, S. P. Chaudhuri, trans., Imperial Bureau of Soil Science 59 (England, 1926); P. M. Cato and M. T. Varo, *On Agriculture*, T. D. Page, ed. (Cambridge, Mass.: Harvard University Press, 1960).

13. S. A. Waksman, op. cit.

14. *Encyclopedia Brittanica: Micropaedia*, 15th ed., vol. 5, pp. 207, 973; D. P. Hopkins, *Chemicals, Humus and the Soil*, op. cit., pp. 14–17; M. M. Kononova, "Humus of the Main soil Types and Soil Fertility," in *Organic Matter and Soil Fertility* (Amsterdam, North Holland Publ., 1968), pp. 361–379; S. A. Waksman, op. cit., pp. xi–xii.

15. M. Alexander, "Degradation of Natural and Synthetic Organic Compounds in Soils," *Organic Matter and Soil Fertility*, pp. 511–534; N. R. Dhar, "The Value of Organic Matter, Phosphates, and Sunlight Nitrogen Fixation and Fertility Improved in World Soils," op. cit., pp. 242–360; W. Flaig, op. cit., S. A. Waksman, op. cit., p. xii.

16. W. A. J. Flaig, "Uptake of Organic Substances from Soil Organic Matter by Plants and Their Influences on Metabolism," *Organic Matter and Soil Fertility*, pp. 722–776; D. P. Hopkins, op. cit., p. 12; A. L. Page and L. P. Bratt, "Effects of Sewage Sludge or Effluent Application to Soil on the Movement of Nitrogen, Phosphorous, Soluble Salts and Trace Elements to Ground Waters (Rockville, Md.: Information Transfer, Inc., 1975); S. A. Waksman, op. cit., pp. 406–407.

17. M. Alexander, op. cit.; W. A. J. Flaig, op. cit., S. L. Jansen, op. cit., pp. 123-125.

18. M. Cohen, *The Food Crisis in Prehistory* op. cit., pp. 48-51; D. P. Hopkins, op. cit., pp. 138-146.

19. Interested readers should consult G. E. Fussell, *Farming Techniques from Prehistoric to Modern Times*; J. Fritsch, *The Manufacturing of Chemical Manures* (London: Scott Greenwood & Sons, 1911); A. D. Hall, *Fertilizer and Manures* (New York: Macmillan, 1914); A. I. McKay, *Farming and Gardening in the Bible* (Emmaus, Pa.: Rodale Press, 1950); F. H. King, *Farmers for Forty Centuries* (New York: Harcourt, Brace, 1927); W. Hinton, *Fanshen* (New York: Vintage Books, 1966); G. W. Cooke, *Fertilizer and Society* (London: Fertilizer Society of London, 1971); H. J. Wheeler, *Manures and Fertilizers* (New York: Macmillan, 1914); Mather and Hart, op. cit.

20. R. Blobaum, "China Recycles Her Wastes....", in *Compost Science* 16 no. 5 (1975), pp. 16-19; W. Rybcynski, "Appropriate Sanitation for the World's Poor," *Compost Science* 18 no. 4 (1977): 10-12; A. Rockefeller, "Private Profit and Public Waste: The Connection," *Compost Science* 17 no. 4 (1976), pp. 13-15. Michael Perelman, "Politics, Prices and Priorities, Toward a Rational Use of Our Resources," *Compost Science* 18 no. 1, (1977) pp. 31-32; Jeff Cox, "The Economic Value of Organic Matter in Crop Production," *Compost Science* 16 no. 5 (1975): 24-25; J. Busterud, "The Economic Impact of Environmental Regulation," *Hearings Before the Joint Economic Committee*, 93rd Congress, 2nd Session, Nov. 19, 21 and 22, 1974, p. 130.

21. Human body waste treated with some other material high in cellulose, such as sawdust or leaves. See Parasara Mamumi, op. cit., S. C. Bernerji et al., eds., Krsi-Parasara, *Bibliotheca Indica*, vol. 285 (1960); *The Bible*, Daniel, op. cit., Luke 14: 35; Nehemia 11: 13 and 12: 31; J. C. Scott, *Health and Agriculture in China* (London: Faber & Faber, 1953), chaps. 11-14; T. D. Hinesly, *Agricultural Benefits and Environmental Changes Resulting from the Use of Digested Sludge on Field Crops*, EPA Report PB-236, 402 (1974); FAO, *Organic Materials as Fertilizers*, op. cit.; *China: Recycling of Organic Wastes in Agriculture*, Soils Bulletin 40 (Rome, 1978); OECD, *Effective Use of Fertilizers* (Paris, 1957); FAO, *Organic Materials and Soil Productivity*, Soils Bulletin 35 (Rome, 1977); H. J. Wheeler, op. cit., pp. 10-18; F. H. King, *Farmers of Forty Centuries* (New York: Harcourt, Brace, 1927), pp. 71-80; W. Hinton, op. cit., p. 23ff.

22. In addition to the items cited in ref. 21 above, see also R. L. Chaney, "Crop and Food Chain Effects of Toxic Elements in Sludges and Effluents," in *Recycling Municipal Sludges and Effluents on Land* (Washington, D.C.: National Association of State Universities and Land Grant Colleges, 1973), 129-141; Anon., "Sanitary Effects of Urban Garbage and Night Soil Composting," *Chinese Medical Journal* 6 (November 1975): 407-412; "How Farmers Can Reduce Fertilizer Bills by Using On-Farm Wastes and Urban Sludge," *Compost Science* (March-June, 1975): A. C. Garg, op. cit., pp. 15-33; C. Göllueke, *Composting* (Emmaus, Pa.: Rodale Press, 1973), pp. 13-49; Sir Albert Howard, *The Soil and Health* (New York: Devin-Adair Co., 1947), pp. 209, 274.

23. See Table 5.1. Estimates are based on data and definitions in J. B. Lawes, op. cit., pp. 18–27; FAO, *Organic Materials as Fertilizers*, op. cit., pp. 20–24; A. C. Garg, op. cit., pp. 9–10; 47–48; D. P. Burkitt (1971 and 1972); Rendtorf and Kashagarian, op. cit., P. J. Cammidge (1914), op. cit., and Sunderman and Boerner, op. cit.
24. Compare the figures in Tables 5.3 and 5.4.
25. Table 5.1.
26. See Tables 5.1, 8.3–8.7.

FURTHER READING

Balfour, E. B. *The Living Soil*. London: Faber & Faber, 1942.

Colonna, R. A., & McLaren, C. *Decision Maker's Guide in Solid Waste Management*. Washington, Environmental Protection Agency, 1974.

Darwin, C. *On Humus and Earthworms*. London, 1881.

Devik, O. *Harvesting Polluted Waters*. New York: Plenum Press, 1976.

Eglinton, G., ed. *Organic Geochemistry*. New York: Springer-Verlag, 1969.

FAO/IAEA. *The Use of Isotopes in Soil Organic Matter Studies*. Report of FAO, IAEA Technical Meeting. New York: Oxford University Press, 1966.

Furon, R., *The Problem of Water: A World Study*. New York: American Elsvier Publishing Company, 1967.

Gorsuch, T. T. *The Destruction of Organic Matter*. Oxford: Pergamon Press, 1970.

Gloyna, E. *Waste Stabilization Ponds*. Geneva: WHO, 1971.

Hawkes, H. A. *The Ecology of Waste Water Treatment*. New York: Pergamon Press, 1963.

Hynes, H. B. N. *The Biology of Polluted Waters*. Liverpool: Liverpool University Press, 1966.

McLaren, A. D., ed. *Soil Biochemistry*. New York: Marcel Dekker, Inc., 1967.

Mechalas, B. *A Study of Nitrification and Denitrification*. Cincinnati: Advanced Waste Water Treatment Research Laboratory, 1970.

Parkinson, D., ed. *The Ecology of Soil Fungi*. Liverpool: Liverpool University Press, 1960.

Pauli, F. W. "Humus and Plant," (the direct humus effect) in *Science Progress* 59 (1961): 427–439.

Peterson, J. R., et. al., "Human & Animal Wastes as Fertilizers" in *Fertilizer Technology and Use*, 2nd ed. Madison, Wisconsin: Soil Science Society of America, 1971.

Purvis, J. E. *The Chemical Examination of Water, Sewage, Food, and Other Substances.* Cambridge: Cambridge University Press, 1914.

Rodale, J. I. *The Organic Front.* Emmaus, Pa.: Rodale Press, 1949.

Schnifzer, M., and Khan, S. U., *Humic Substances in the Environment.* New York: Marcel Dekker, Inc., 1972.

Soil Science Terms. Madison Wisconsin: SSSA, 1975.

Stoner, Carol H. *Alternatives to Cess Pools, Septic Tanks and Sewers.* Emmaus, Pa.: Rodale Press, 1977.

Sykes, F. *Humus and the Farmer.* London: Faber & Faber, 1946.

U. K. Cabinet Office. *Future World Trends.* London: HMSO, 1976.

USDA. *Wastes in Relation to Agriculture and Forestry.* Washington: United States Environmental Protection Agency, 1974.

Van Vuren, J. P. J. *Soil Fertility and Sewage.* New York: Dover Publishers Inc., 1948.

Wadham, S. M. *The Humus Controversy.* Brisbane: Royal Australian College of Physics, 1948.

PART III: PROSPECTS:
Material Reconversion, Economic Value, and Utilization of Human Waste

6

THE EMERGENCE OF BODY WASTE FERTILIZERS

Experience of users of organic manures has indicated that the quality of crops, particularly fruits and vegetables, is superior to the quality obtained with chemical fertilizers. It would be useful to obtain some conclusive experimental evidence on this aspect. . . .*

The use of night soil and animal dung in agriculture and for fertilizing crops predates written history.[1] This practice was known not only to early Greeks and Romans but also to the Chinese, the Japanese, and the Indians whose use of such items goes back several millennia.[2] It is important to note that in comparatively recent history, "night soil is husbanded in almost every part of Europe, particularly on the continent, with a jealousy and care which proves how valuable it is considered by those who use it."[3] The total demand for body waste fertilizers was such that "it is a source of profit, first to the householder; second, to the night man, who carts it away; and

*A. C. Garg, et al., *Organic Manures* ICAR Bulletin 32 (New Delhi: ICAR, 1971), p. 46.

thirdly, to the farmer, who is the last purchaser and who applies it to his land."[4] At the dawn of the nineteenth century, processed night soil of varying composition was marketed in Europe and America under the general name "poudrette."[5] At that time in history civilization's attitude about night soil and the use of body waste nutrients for increasing the productivity of the soil was essentially the same in both hemispheres.[6] By the second half of the nineteenth century, however, significant changes in the method of handling body waste had taken place in the West. New techniques leading to the water-carriage system were introduced and effected in expedient fashion, including development of the water closet, the construction of drain-sewers, and, finally, the water-carriage sewage and waste treatment systems.[7] The social impact of these engineering projects has been most beneficial in higher standards of sanitation and public health. Yet, on examination of the direct and indirect social costs one hundred years later, the ecological disadvantages are of great concern. The negative side effects range from varying degrees of locally harmful pollution of soil, water, and air, to major environmental damages of catastrophic proportions. Although the water-carriage system serves its limited purposes, the related problem of absorption posed by sewage sludge and effluent are more complex to solve than that of body waste disposal alone, because of the presence of certain inorganic elements (some of which may be toxic to plant and animal life) in sewage by-products. Historically, four different methods of common disposal—burning, burying, dumping (on high seas and in community waters) and recycling or combinations thereof—have been and are being applied all over the world. The population explosion, with the concomitant problems of severe food shortage and fecal pollution, makes it all the more imperative for us to consider the possibilities offered by agronutrient recovery through body waste recyling. Body waste and other organic substances had been used by individuals to increase the productivity of the soil for several millennia before the use of municipal sewage in irrigation began in England in the nineteenth century.[8] Before

1890, several European countries, including Germany, Austria, France, and Italy, authorized the operation of raw sewage farms. In selected areas of the United States, the establishment of farms using raw sewage also began in the late nineteenth century.[9] In most instances, the primary goals of countries using sewage for irrigation[10] included the confinement of wastewater on land, and utilization of the fertilizing value of sewage nutrients. In practical terms, however, the national objectives of securing public health safety and maximization of the fertilizing value of sewage were often in conflict then, as they are today.[11]

Although sewage regulation standards and practice vary widely in different parts of the world, the basic standards are generally formulated to achieve the following goals: a) adequate protection of the public from the transmission of enteric diseases caused by intestinal pathogenic bacteria and animal parasites; b) prevention of public nuisance and ground water pollution; and c) protection of farm workers. From the point of view of technical applications, most comprehensive irrigation practice requires mechanical pretreatment, plus sedimentary, chemical, and biological treatments. For example, European sewage irrigation practice requires mechanical pretreatment, and then sedimentation with a one- to two-hour detention period.[12] In the United States, however, sewage irrigation standards are directed primarily toward water reclamation and ignore the potential fertilization value. In view of the prevailing differences in social valuation of sewage materials, it is important to note that "esthetic considerations are much more important here (i.e., the United States) than in Europe where sewage farming may be considered an economic necessity."[13]

THE EFFICIENCY OF BODY WASTE FERTILIZERS

The fertilizing value of organic matter has been clearly demonstrated by its natural capacity to supply varying amounts of soil nutrients (humus) and plant nutrients (NPK compounds) in various climates, soil conditions, and methods of cultivation which prevail in different countries. The result of numerous field and experimental studies indicate that body waste fertilizers, like animal manures, offer organic substances in different stages of decomposition which can productively and profitably be utilized in agriculture.[14] In a number of countries, both solid and liquid varieties (sludge and effluent) of body waste fertilizers are in common use and their effects on the yield of agronomic crops have been beneficial.[15] The response of crops such as cotton, sorghum, wheat, sugar cane, and potatoes to body waste fertilizers has been particularly satisfactory.[16] By comparing today's crop yields, on the one hand, and the projected (estimated) costs of organic body waste agronutrients in relation to inorganic chemical fertilizers on the other, one obtains the required basis at the micro level to judge whether the user cost of body waste fertilizers will increase or decrease the existing gap between its private and social profitability. But because of its multiple beneficial effects on society at large, the efficiency of body waste fertilizers must be evaluated at the macro (i.e., environmental) rather than the micro (i.e., agricultural enterprise) level. As long as the objectives of individual countries are the achievement of the maximum agricultural production at the lowest possible price, the unappropriability of the total external economic benefits of using body waste fertilizers to individual farmers will continue to militate against optimal use of these fertilizers, thereby radically favoring the continued application of inorganic chemical fertilizers.

In discussing the efficiency of body waste fertilizers, it is important to underline the fact that there are different varieties that range from night soil compost to digested sludge.[17] The effects of body waste fertilizers on the chemical composition of soil, plant and water depends, among other things, on the biological stability of the kinds used. Numerous investigators have pointed out that the night soil compost as well as the digested sludge can be an effective source of Nitrogen-

Phosphorous-Potassium for crop fertilization, under appropriate rates of application with certain limited exceptions.[18] Acknowledging for the moment the demonstrable efficiency of digested sludge in increasing the production of good-quality crops, that approach to the body waste disposal problem may be reasonable only for those countries which are unalterably locked into the water-carriage sewage collection and treatment system. Unfortunately, it is a solution which, judging from the prevailing global condition, appears to be of limited relevance and general applicability. What the overwhelming majority of the countries needs now is a general solution to the body waste problem which includes appropriate techniques for "digested night soil" fertilizers. What science has already accomplished for raw sewage, it must now achieve for night soil management in nonsewered areas and heavily populated areas.[19] The first phase of a general solution could begin with a crash program to develop the counterpart of a synthetic technology for "digested night soil" similar to the Japanese prototype, to produce agronutrients; with a proviso that the quality of plant foods produced by this process would, at least, match the biological stability and crop production efficiency of the most effective "digested sewage sludge." A complete specification of technical possibilities based on variable combinations of the production functions for "digested night soil" and "digested sewage sludge" should subsequently be undertaken. The working data so derived will provide a set of analytical solutions of general applicability, so that the maximum range of application of the two combined systems will offer individual countries better options to realize substantial benefits from international cooperation aimed at maximizing the total objectives of a global solution to the body waste problem. The immediate short-term goal of the phase one program is to produce a wide variety of acceptable, but not necessarily perfect, solutions. This limited task is obviously a precondition to the second phase: the final long-term global solution. Although it is not an end in itself, the accomplishment even of the phase one program would represent a marked improvement on the deplorable conditions prevailing in pre-phase one world. A successful conclusion of phase one tasks would facilitate the implementation of the phase two program by offering adequate combinations of supportive and indispensable factors such as effective technology, material resources, and time opportunity. The long-term global solution envisaged in the phase two program will not only eliminate the residual problems in phase one (including the social impact of viral agents, pathogenic organisms, and heavy metals associated with the use of body waste agronutrients), but also will enhance the maximization of crop production efficiency achieved through the application of processed body waste plant nutrients.

BODY WASTE FERTILIZERS:
PUBLIC HEALTH AND POLLUTION PROBLEMS

In using body waste fertilizers, a widespread source of concern is the potential incidence of disease from pathogenic organisms and/or toxic metallic trace elements incorporated in soils, crops, and waters. Heavy metals such as zinc, cadmium, copper and lead, as well as pathogenic bacteria such as Ascaris lumbricoides, Taenia saginala, and tubercle bacilli and fecal coliforms, are well-known constituents of treated sewage. For the most part, the toxic and nontoxic elements occuring as constituents of sludge are traceable to waste materials discharged by various chemical-based industrial processes. Results from studies conducted in England and the United States indicate that most waste treatment plant sludges contain higher concentrations of certain metallic elements, including Cd, Cv, Cu, Pb, Hg, Zn than are found in typical agricultural soils.[20] From various measurements and analyses of extractable concentrations of trace elements in sludges, investigations suggest that when sludges are utilized for crop fertilization over a period of several years, some of the accumulating elements may cause toxicity problems in plants that could lead to deleterious effects on the health of those eating the crops.

Concerning pathogenic organisms in processed body waste, the fact that sewage sludge contains a large population of fecal coliforms renders it suspect as a potential vector of bacterial pathogens and a possible contaminant of soil, water, and air, not to mention crops. Numerous investigations in different parts of the world have confirmed the presence of intestinal pathogenic bacteria and animal parasites in sewage, sludge, and fecal materials.[21] The range of subjects covered in these studies is comprehensive and includes the effects of sewage-polluted irrigation water on vegetables, survival times of pathogenic organisms (such as salmonella, ascaris, shigella, helminth eggs, brucella, leptospira) in rivers and lakes, and comparative densities of bacteria in varying degrees of water pollution. The widening scope of public interest in such studies is more than academic. In the fields of disease prevention and control, epidemiological evidence indicates that vegetables irrigated with sewage or sewage-polluted water have caused many communicable diseases in many parts of the world.[22]

The preceding problem reveals some of the underlying conflicts between the use of the fertilizing powers of body waste nutrients and the necessity to secure adequate standards of public health. The need for basic procedures to protect public health, however, need not preclude the use of body waste fertilizers under acceptable standards of safety. In this connection, several investigations of the survival patterns of pathogenic organisms have demonstrated the possibility of stabilizing fecal materials through successive applications of appropriate aerobic and anaerobic processes.[23] The problems of disease prevention and control are surmountable if the appropriate combinations of research efforts and supportive field work can be effected. It is now sufficiently clear that the solution to these problems will require an optimal coordination of agricultural, environmental, and public health programs.

NOTES

1. For selected references see Mamuni Parasara, *Krishi Sangraha*, S. P. Chaudhuri, trans., Imperial Bureau of Soil Science 59 (England, 1926); also KRSI-PARASARA, S. C. Bernerji and G. P. Majundar, eds. and trans., in *Bibliotecha Indica*, vol. 285 (1960); *The Bible*: Daniel 2:5 and 3:20, Luke 4:35, and Nehemiah 2:13 and 12:31.
2. *Krisni Sangraha*, op. cit.; F. H. King, *Farmers for Forty Centuries* (New York: Harcourt, Brace, 1927); P. M. Cato and M. T. Varo, *On Agriculture*, ed. T. D. Page (Cambridge, Mass.: Harvard University Press, 1960).
3. D. J. Browne, *American Muck Book* (New York: C. M. Saxon, 1851), p. 302.
4. Ibid.
5. Ibid., p.. 305–312.
6. W. H. Corfield, *Treatment and Utilization of Sewage* (New York: Macmillan & Co., 1887), pp. 64–67.
7. Ibid., chapters 5, 6 and 7.
8. Ibid., chapter 11; D. H. Browne, op. cit., pp. 337–349; E. S. Chase, "Nine Decades of Sanitary Engineering," *Water Works and Wastes Engineering* vol. 1 (1964), pp. 48–49.
9. R. Stone, "Land Disposal of Sewage and Industrial Wastes," S. I. W. 25 (1953) 406; E. N. Chapman, "Sewage Contaminated Water," *American Journal of Public Health 25* (1935): 930; C. Wright, "Pollution of Irrigation Water," S. I. W. 22 (1950): 403.
10. For example, see T. A. Lambo, "The Protection and Improvement of the World's Drinking Water Quality" in *Biological Control of Water Pollution* (Philadelphia: University of Pennsylvania Press, 1976), pp. 22–29; Zunker, "Land Treatment of Sewage and Agriculture" Ber. Abwassert, Ver. 7, 113 (1956), WPA 16 (1950); N. Litvinov, "Water Pollution in the USSR and in Other Eastern European Countries," *WHO Bull.* 26 (1962), p. 439; A. Key, "Pollution of Surface Waters in Europe," *WHO Bull.* 14 (1956), p. 839.
11. G. R. Stewart, *Not So Rich As You Think* (Boston: Houghton Mifflin Co., 1958), chapter 4.
12. W. Muller, "Ascaris Eggs in Sewage and Their Durability in Digestion Tanks," *Water Pollution Abstract* 2290 (1956); B. L. Muller, "Results of Investigations of the Content of Worm Eggs in the Irrigation Districts of North Leipzig and Delitz," *Water Pollution Abstract* 1697 (1956); G. Schmauder, "Examination and Considerations for the Hygiene of Land Utilization of Sewage," Wasserw-Wassertech 93 (1957), p. 71; H. Kruse, "Some Present Day Sewage Treatment Methods in Use for Small Communities in the Federal Republic of Germany," *WHO Bull.* 26 (1962); 542; A. Kreuz, "Hygienic Evaluation of the Agricultural Utilization of Sewage," *Water Pollution Abstract* 161 (1956); T. Bush, "Agricultural Use of Sewage, Its Position in the Water Management and Technical and Hygienic Problems" 10 (Berlin: Institute f. Wasserwirtschaft, 1960).
13. Endel Sepp, "The Use of Sewage for Irrigation," Bulletin of Sanitary Engineering (California State Dept. of Public Health, July 1963), p. 15: A.

Kreuz, op. cit.; L. V. Wilcox, "Agricultural Uses of Reclaimed Sewage Effluent," *Sewage Works Journal* 20 (1948): 24; G. Schmauder, op. cit.

14. FAO, *China, Recycling of Organic Wastes in Agriculture* (Rome, 1978); T. D. Hinesley, *Agricultural Benefits and Environmental Changes Resulting from the Use of Digested Sludge on Field Crops*, Environmental Protection Agency (Washington, D.C.: 1974); FAO, *Organic Material as Fertilizers*, Soils Bulletin 27 (Rome, 1975); OECD, *Effective Use of Fertilizers* (Paris, 1957), pp. 177–186; S. Z. Hershkovitz and A. Feinwesser, *Management of Nutrients on Agricultural Land*, EPA (Washington, D.C.: GPO, 1971), pp. 79–80; O. E. Cross, "Animal Waste Utilization for Pollution Abatement-Technology and Economics," Project Report, Water Resources Research Institute (Lincoln, Neb.: University of Nebraska, 1974).

15. S. A. Hershkovitz and A. Feinwesser, "Utilization of Sewage for Agricultural Purposes," *Water and Sewage Works* vol. 114 (1967), pp. 181–184; A. D. Day and T. C. Tucker, "Production of Small Grain Pasture Forage . . ." *Agronomy Journal* 51 (1959): 569; T. D. Hinesly, "Agricultural Application of Digested Sewage Sludge" in *Municipal Sewage Effluent for Irrigation* (Ruston, La.: Louisiana Polytechnical Institute, 1968); E. O. Dyl, "Crop Irrigation with Sewage Effluent," *Sewage and Industrial Wastes* 29 (1957), pp. 825–828; H. Henkelek, "Utilization of Sewage for Crop Irrigation in Israel," *Sewage and Industrial Wastes* 29 (1957), pp. 868–874; A. C. Garg et al., *Organic Manures* (New Delhi: Indian Council of Agricultural Research, 1971); FAO, *Organic Materials and Soil Productivity*, Soils Bulletin 35 (Rome: 1977).

16. Corfield, op. cit., pp. 411–421; F. I. C. Jackson and Y. D. Wad, "The Sanitary Disposal and Agricultural Utilization of Habitation Wastes by the Indore Process," *The Indian Medical Gazette* (February 1934); 93–100; S. R. Aldrich in *Fact from Environment* (Atlanta, Georgia: American Potash Institute), p. 12; T. D. Hinesly, op. cit.; G. C. W. Ames, "Can Organic Manures Improve Crop Production in Southern India?" *Compost Science* 17 no. 2 (1976), pp. 7–18; R. E. Sjoren, "Application of Sewage Sludge to Garden Plots," *Compost Science* 18 no. 5 (1977), pp. 26–32; FAO, *Organic Materials and Soil Productivity*.

17. FAO, *China* . . .; J. C. Scott, op. cit., chapter 11, 12 and 14; T. D. Hinesly, op. cit., LA/OMA Project Report, *Sludge Processing and Disposal*, USEPA and California State Water Resources Control Board (1977); A. C. Garg et al., op. cit.; FAO, *Organic Materials and Soil Productivity*.

18. It must be noted, however, that with special regard to its nutrients supplying capacity, the relative proportion of potassium to nitrogen and phosphorous contained in body waste fertilizers may be inadequate for growing crops in potassium-deficient soils. J. C. Scott, op. cit.; FAO, *China*, op. cit., T. D. Hinesly, op. cit., LA/OMA Project report, op. cit.; FAO, *Organic Materials and Soil Productivity*.

19. The Japanese night soil digester program is a forerunner in this direction.

20. T. D. Hinesly, op. cit., pp. 17; see also M. L. Berrow and J. Webber, "Trace Elements in Sewage Sludge," *Journal of the Science of Food and Agriculture* 23 (1972), p. 93; D. Purves, "Consequences of Trace-Element Contamination of Soils," *Environmental Pollution* 3 (1972), p. 17.

21. W. Rudolphs et. al., "Literature Review on the Occurrence and Survival of Enteric, Pathogenic, and Relative Organisms in Soil, Water, Sewage and Sludges, and on Vegetation" 1: Bacterial and Virus Diseases, *Sewage and Industrial Wastes* 22 (1950), p. 1261, and 2: Animal Parasites, Idem, 22 (1950), p. 1417; A. Kreuz, op. cit., W. Rudolphs et al, "Contamination of Vegetables Grown in Polluted Soil," *Sewage and Industrial Wastes* 23 (1951), pp. 253ff, 478ff, 656ff and 992ff; C. T. Wright, "Pollution of Irrigation Waters," *Wet Sewage and Industrial Wastes* 22 (1950), p. 1403; C. O. Melick, "The Possibility of Typhoid Infection Through Vegetables: *Journal of Infectious Diseases* 21 (July 1917), p. 38; F. L. Morse, "Report of Medical Inspector," Massachusetts State Board of Health Rep. 34 (1899), p. 761; Indian Institute of Science 1938–1948, "Investigations on Sewage Farming," p. 50; R. M. Worth, "Rural Health in China: From Village to Commune," *American Journal of Hygiene* 77 (May 1963): 228; A. Key, "Pollution of Surface Waters in Europe," *WHO Bull.* 14 (1956), p. 839; J. C. Scott, *Health and Agriculture in China* (London: Faber & Faber, Ltd., 1953).

22. For a review of the literature on this subject, see Endel Sepp, op cit.; see also: T. G. Hanks, *Solid Waste/Disease Relationships: A Literature Survey*, U.S. Public Health Service Report SW-1C; J. R. Miner et al., "*Salmonella infantis* in Cattle Feedlot Runoff," in *Applied Microbiology* 15:627–628; S. L. Diesch, *Survival of Pathogens in Animal Manure Disposal*, E. P. A. (Washington, D.C.: GPO, 1973); J. W. Messer, et al., "An Assessment of some Public Health Problems Resulting From Feeding Poultry Litter to Animals," in *Poultry Science* 50: 874–881; M. L. Peterson, *Parasitological Examination of Compost*, E.P.A. Solid Waste Research Open-File Report (Cincinnati: Office of Research & Monitoring, 1971).

23. T. D. Hinesly, *Agricultural Benefits and Environmental Changes . . .*, pp. 8–11; see also R. F. Goudey, "New Thoughts on Sludge Digestion and Sludge Disposal," *Sewage Works Journal* 4 (1932) p. 609; R. L. Irgens and H. O. Halvorson, "Removal of Plant Nutrients by Means of Aerobic Stabilization of Sludge," *Applied Microbiology* 13 no. 3 (1965) p. 373; H. A. Lunt, *Digested Sewage Sludge for Soil Improvement*, Connecticut Experiment Station Bulletin 622 (1959) pp. 1–30; T. D. Hinesly, et al., "Liquid Fertilizer to Reclaim Land and Produce Crops," *Water Research* 6 (1972) p. 545; T. Viraragharan, "Digesting Sludge by Aeration," *Water Works and Wastes Engineering* 2, no. 9 (1965) p. 86; H. W. Wolf, "Housefly Breeding in Sewage Sludge," *Sewage and Industrial Wastes* 27, no. 2 (1955) p. 172; F. G. Pohland, *General Review of Literature on Anaerobic Sewage Sludge Digestion*, Engineering Extension Bulletin, Series no. 110 (Lafayette: Purdue University 1967); FAO, *China,*; J. C. Scott, op. cit.; FAO *Organic Materials as Fertilizers*.

FURTHER READING

Economics of Sludge Applications Systems on Agricultural Lands, Ag West Inc., Davis, Ca., 1974.

FAO, *Organic Materials as Fertilizers*, Soils Bulletin 27. Rome, 1975.

———. *Organic Material and Soil Productivity*. Soils Bulletin 35. Rome, 1977.

———. *Organic Recycling in Asia and the Pacific*. Soils Bulletin. Rome, 1978.

Goldstein, J. *Sensible Sludge:* A New Look at a Wasted Resource. Emmaus, Pa.: Rodale Press, 1977.

Golueke, C. *Biological Reclamation of Solid Wastes*. Emmaus, Pa.: Rodale Press, 1977.

———. *Composting*. Emmaus, Pa.: Rodale Press, 1972.

Kapp, K. W. "Recycling in Contemporary China," in *World Development*, vol. 3 (July–August, 1975).

Salvato, J. A. *Environmental Sanitation*. New York: John Wiley & Sons, 1958.

Venkataraman. *Algal Bio-fertilizers for Rice Cultivation*. New Delhi: Indian Agricultural Research Institute, 1977.

7

BODY WASTE MANAGEMENT SYSTEMS: AN OVERVIEW

Anyone starting out from scratch to plan a civilization would hardly have designed such a monster as our collective sewage system. Its existence gives additional point to the sometimes asked question, Is there any evidence of intelligent life on the planet Earth?

G. R. Stewart*

There are a large number of ways to approach the problem of body waste management. The preferred local solutions should offer the greatest possible benefit to the public by promoting nationwide reclamation for increased crop yields while, at the same time, effectively reducing the incident of fecal-borne diseases. The examples to be examined in this section are selected for only illustrative purposes rather than for specific product recommendation. Because of wide environmental differences and other factors, the choice of applicable techniques will vary between local areas and among different countries. Therefore a comparative review of extant representa-

Not So Rich As You Think (Boston: Houghton Mifflin Co., 1958), p. 41.

tive processes is essential for a better understanding of their technical and practical possibilities.

Waste management systems are generally composed of a number of processes, most of which are involved in waste treatment and in some materials recovery. In general, the essential mechanism in any system is the method of oxidation whereby actual conversion of processing takes place. Oxidation of the waste material can be accomplished in a number of ways which, for purposes of discussion, may be grouped under three major headings: the biological, chemical, and physical processes. *The biological processes* include a wide range of biotic systems of which aerobic stabilization, anaerobic digestion, and direct algal production are well-known examples. *The chemical processes* are comprised of a variety of chemical treatment systems such as chlorination and lime stabilization. *The physical processes* are combined systems in which chemical reagents such as molecular oxygen are employed with the necessary physical treatment to produce the proper temperature and pressure required for waste treatment. Other examples of physical processes are incineration, pyrolysis, dewatering, and wet oxidation techniques.

BIOLOGICAL PROCESSES

An environmentally sound disposal of processed body waste requires that concentrated organic solids first be stabilized. Stabilization processes destroy volatile solids, minimize putrescibility, eliminate most pathogenic organisms, and reduce waste moisture content. Biological processes commonly employed for stabilization include anaerobic and aerobic digestion.

Anaerobic digestion is a biochemical method of waste stabilization in which a variety of anaerobic and facultative anaerobic organisms participate simultaneously in assimilating and decomposing organic matter. In this process, the specialized activity of the acid-forming organisms and the methane-forming bacteria are combined to convert the complex organic substrate to low molecular-weight organic acids and the volatile organic acids to methane. There are three types of anaerobic digester systems in use: the "single-stage," the "two-stage" digesters for sewage sludge, and the night soil digester. The capital costs of the respective units may range between an estimated $4,000 for the night soil digester (based on Indian and Japanese prototypes)[1] to at least $1.5 million for the sewage sludge digesters.[2]

Energy is an important input in any anaerobic digestion process. It is required in most phases of the process for mixing the contents of the digester, maintaining gas recirculation, heating the incoming sludge, and maintaining the appropriate temperature. On the output side, some of the major advantages of anaerobic digestion are its by-products: digester gas (with a heat value of approximately 600 Btu/Cuft.), and a stabilized digester sludge.[3] The methane gas and sludge thus produced are of increasing interest in the current energy crisis and the chronic shortage of fertilizer in many parts of the world.

The aerobic digestion process is an extension of the aerobic method, with a wider range of application to intermediate waste materials.[4] In typical operations, the mixture of intermediate materials to be stabilized is supplied to the digester, oxygen is added, and the necessary mixing of the digester is achieved with mechanical aerators. At the completion of processing, sufficient time is allowed for supernatant to be decanted and for sludge solids to settle before subsequent disposal.

Like the anaerobic digestion process, energy is required also in aerobic digestion to supply oxygen with which to effect the stabilization of th sludge delivered to the system. Although there is a paucity of cost data for the aerobic digester,[5] some of the available information indicates a significant variation in fixed (i.e., capital inputs) and variable (i.e., operation and management inputs) costs components.[6] Consequently, direct cost comparisons between aerobic and anaerobic digestion systems are difficult, if not impossible. One reference stated, however, that "Capital costs for aerobic digestion are lower than anaerobic digestion."[7] Lower capital costs in aerobic digestion are probably due to several factors that include the additional expenses of insulation, heating equipment, and special covers that are required by an aerobic digestion. Compared to other forms of biological stabilization systems, the aerobic composting and digestion processes are receiving widespread attention in both developed and developing countries as effective methods of converting body waste into agronutrients.

CHEMICAL PROCESSES

Lime and chlorine are two basic compounds which are active in the chemical stabilization processes examined below.

Lime Stabilization

Body waste materials which are not biologically or physically digested can be rendered biologically stable, pending final disposal, by the addition of lime. This method of treatment is usually considered a temporary stabilization procedure. In typical operations, lime is most frequently used as a measure of last resort in overloaded plants or at facilities experiencing digester problems. According to most technical specifications, dosage levels of lime required to achieve and maintain the critical pH factor (e.g., 11.5) depend on the alkalinity of the body waste material.[8] In order to achieve satisfactory lime stabilization, lime must be hydrated or slaked before application.

Based on the average values of inputs, the estimated costs of construction, operations, and management, including special expenses for lime slaking and feeding equipment, range between $100,000 and $1.5 million.[9] One of the basic drawbacks of the lime stabilization process, despite its temporary biologically stabilizing effect on body waste, is that lime is not an oxidizing agent. This fact explains why no direct oxidation of organic matter takes place and why the treated body waste material is not chemically stabilized. For example, if the pH factor of the stabilized body waste material should drop below the critical minimum, surviving bacteria could revive, multiply, and repeat their natural cycle. Notwithstanding these technical qualifications, a biologically stable body waste material effected by lime stabilization is not precluded from suitable agricultural application.

Chlorine Stabilization

In conventional waste treatment with chemicals, chlorine is one of the compounds employed for oxidizing the organic matter present in body waste.[10] Oxidation products recoverable from chlorine stabilization include humus and certain trace elements suitable for utilization in agriculture. In normal situations, it requires a 200-mg dose of chlorine to oxidize and destroy most biological activity in body waste materials.[11] Being mostly free from the basic drawbacks of lime, chlorine-stabilized sludge is considered stable and reported to dewater readily on sand beds with no unpleasant odors.

The expense of chlorination varies directly with "the amount of sludge to be chemically oxidized and the chlorine dosage."[12] In 1976, for example, the estimated cost of chlorine was approximately $200/ton. Despite its demonstrated effectiveness as an oxidizing agent, massive applications of chlorine in processing body waste may produce a variety of negative environmental side effects that include possible formation of chlorinated organics and possible toxicity to fish and other aquatic life.

PHYSICAL PROCESSES

Compared to other conventional waste treatment systems (e.g., the biological or chemical processes), *incineration and pyrolysis* are processes used to reduce the volume and mass of body waste solids as well as to sterilize the processed materials. The *incineration* itself consists of two separate operations, viz: volatization of body waste and combustion of the volatized material. Volatization and combustion may be done in separate pieces of equipment or successively in the same unit. Suppliers of equipment for the industry have developed a wide variety of incineration machines based on the three principal types of incinerating systems: the multiple earth, the fluidized bed, and the flash drier-incinerator.[13] The use of incineration has grown since it was introduced over half a century ago. A team of experts pointed out in a recent study that "one of the reasons for the growth of sludge incineration has been the decrease in land availability for land disposal alternatives."[14]

Cost factors on incineration systems vary widely depending on, among other things, the type of incinerator and the nature of the material to be incinerated.[15] The combined average cost of capital and operating expenses of existing units are estimated at about $1.5 million. The use of conventional sludge incineration has three drawbacks. The first of these involves pollution and is revealed by increased concern over air-quality standards. The second concern involves economics and is underlined by the increased cost of fuel. The third and final area of concern comes from the need for resource conservation, a growing awareness that sludge is a reusable resource, too valuable to be incinerated. These and other social concerns have led to an expanded search for more efficient alternative solutions to the incineration of body wastes. One such alternative is offered by pyrolysis.

The *pyrolysis process* is a mechanism by which organic portions of waste are converted into lower molecular-weight compounds; for example, extracting coke from coal and charcoal from wood. In production plants, the standard yield and composition of the by-products of pyrolysis are determined by several variables that include the chemical composition of the raw sludge, reactor temperature, heating rate, and the type of pyrolysis reactor activated.[16] Although there are a number of different reactor types that can be used for pyrolysis, the varieties of equipment available can be classified under two basic headings: *direct fired* and *indirect fired*. The essential difference between the two is that in an indirect fired reactor, ". . . the feed stock materials are contained in an enclosed vessel and do not come in direct contact with the heating gases"[17] unlike a direct fired reactor in which ". . . a fraction of the stoichiometric oxygen required by the waste is admitted directly into the fuel feed to liberate the heat required for pyrolysis or gasification."[18]

As functional examples of physical processes, the incineration and pyrolysis techniques are both thermal conversion processes. Advocates of pyrolysis, however, claim it offers three distinct technical advantages over incineration: (1) that "air pollution control requirements are minimized . . ."[19] in a pyrolysis process because "the fuel gas is scrubbed *prior* to the addition of air . . ."[20] thereby considerably reducing the volume of gas to be cleaned; (2) that several by-products (such as heat and gas) which can be used for a variety of energy-related industrial and household purposes are produced from pyrolysis; and (3) that ". . . pyrolysis processes offer the possibility for improved thermal efficiencies . . . [because] . . . exit gas temperatures can be lower than those from an incinerator without the concern over off-gas odors."[21]

The preceding review of the biological, chemical, and physical processes of conventional body waste management techniques will help to identify and perhaps harmonize some of the potentially unavoidable conflicts arising from the structural duality of the problem to be solved, and to demonstrate the severe limitations of the processes being applied. This brief survey of the three branches of the state of the art confirms that the general principle of body waste management in the past century has been predominantly concerned with the application of waste "processing" or "treatment" systems and has virtually neglected the more basic "disposal" problem.

In recent years, the economic, social, and environmental

costs of traditional solutions to body waste management problems have approached disastrous limits, especially in large centers of population.[22] In response to this new situation, public and private agencies are beginning to reexamine the issues and discover more efficient alternative solutions to the age-old problems of body waste management. Although the facts are well established, it is not yet universally recognized that agronutrients recovered from body waste do play a positive role in increasing crop yields by supplying plant nutrients and by improving the physical, chemical, and biological properties of soils. It would appear reasonable for nations in which agricultural underdevelopment and recurrent food shortage are prevalent to take every possible step to ensure the return of body waste agronutrients to the soil, with or without additional supplies of inorganic chemical fertilizers. To achieve such goals of conservational farm policy, the science of agricultural sanitation[23] should be systematically applied, taking local conditions and circumstances fully into account.

It is commonly accepted by soil scientists, biochemists, and farmers that the organic contents of human body waste are a potential source of humus and plant nutrients. Indeed, man benefited from this natural dividend long before scientific explanations of the humification process were known.[24] Although human manures have been used separately and in combination with animal manures in farming through many centuries, they are no longer regarded today as a practical substitute for the synthetic fertilizers, except in some countries where primary waste is in varying degrees restored to the earth as "night soil."[25] Because of the prevailing attitude toward body waste, the material equivalent of millions of metric tons of humic substances are not being utilized in agriculture. Mankind cannot afford this immense wastage.

The gross neglect of human body waste as an alternative source of plant nutrients is generally explained, and often justified, on the grounds of health and economic considerations. It is argued that the task of handling and disposal of human body waste—especially in large population centers—

has always posed serious health and sanitation problems, such as cholera and typhoid diseases.[26] During the first half of the 1800s, after cholera epidemics and other water-borne diseases were linked to excremental water pollution, social demands for the containment and removal of primary waste pollution became a national crusade in London and in other seriously affected European cities. At that stage of human ecological development and perception, the social response to public health crises weighed more heavily than any other factor in determining the origins and subsequent directions of our present technical practices in body waste management. In the ensuing years, the crisis-inspired principles became the corner-stone of social programs. Thus it came about, in the dawn of sanitation awareness, that the achievement of "maximum sanitation" became the universal guiding principle in the handling, treatment, and disposal of human body waste. In view of the gravity of the threat to national health, it is understandable that the overriding goal of public policy in the mid-nineteenth century was the achievement of maximum sanitation. The danger of an outbreak of cholera or typhoid is as real today as it was more than a hundred years ago[27] and preventive social measures are still necessary. Without appearing to throw the baby out with the soiled diaper, however, the choice of technique should reflect an appreciation for the complex forms of biotic and abiotic interdependence underlying socio-ecosystems.

What about the economic arguments against the use of body waste fertilizers? The well-known practical justification for present procedures is the argument that the fertilizer value of human manure (the sewage sludge), per ton, is so low, compared with chemical fertilizers, that it would be un-economical for farmers to return it to the soil.[28] In reply, given the wastage built into the processing equipment, it is absurd to expect sewage sludge to contain appreciable quantities of soluble materials, since the active nutrients are already dissolved in the liquid part of the sewage, leaving in the sludge only the insoluble phosphates and complex forms of nitrogen.

The problem lies in the profligacy of conventional waste treatment processes. Finally, the present evaluation of sludge and fertilizers, based only on the availability of plant nutrients, is not entirely satisfactory as a criterion of public policy. It suppresses the value of other organic by-products of sewage sludge that are highly rated for soil fertility (for example, the humus substances), and it also neglects the basic fact that fertilizers and humus are complements-at-large in virtually all agricultural production functions.[29]

Based on the chemical constituents of the by-products obtained from *standard* sewage treatment processes, there is no doubt that the sewage sludge being produced offers limited amounts of plant nutrients (fertilizers), and the synthetic fertilizer groups do have a case in maintaining that returning sewage sludge to the soil would be uneconomical. But is this really an accurate evaluation? For example, how are the inevitable social costs of handling body waste, whatever the method of disposal, taken into account in evaluating the concept of private cost and profitability? Furthermore, what proportion of the inevitable social costs of handling body waste is to be subtracted from the unit price of body waste fertilizers and/or added to the unit price of equal amounts of synthetic chemical fertilizers, in order to facilitate sound economic comparisons?

The answers to these questions require a more complete assessment of private and social costs/benefits of the material transformation processes involved in making sewage sludge and chemical fertilizers. Given the inevitable social costs of body waste disposal and the danger of environmental pollution, it seems prudent—even if it may not be economical in the narrow sense of private profitability and cost accounting—to transform body waste into organic fertilizers and to pay farmers the appropriate subsidies to use the plant nutrients so recovered.[30] Unlike the conventional systems, the proposed program would facilitate a more sanitary and productive absorption of body waste manure in the socio-ecosystem. As shown in chapters 6 and 11, there is no conclusive evidence that the sludge, if properly applied, is at a long-term competitive disadvantage with chemical fertilizers in physical productivity. Furthermore, the discovery of adverse side effects (sequelae) of the massive application of chemical fertilizers, to be discussed in chapter 10, has led to increased awareness of the potential for ecological damage resulting from current agricultural practices. It must be conceded, in the light of preceding discussions, that the relevant questions clearly transcend the narrow criterion of private profitability.

It is understandable that in an age of sanitation awareness, engineers were "called upon to tackle the problem from one angle only: inoffensive handling 'of primary human waste' at the lowest cost to the 'taxpayer'".[31] Today, as if in blind perpetuation of the iron law of tradition, cities and towns all over the world are—like their forerunners—aiming at the most efficient method of conveying treated and untreated sewage to the nearest lake, river, or sea. In effect, the toilet and the universal sewage pipe lines are "sweeping away all the wastage that man might return to the soil."[32] Wendell Berry's historical view on this issue is of some interest. He stated, in part, that "What may be our largest agricultural waste is not usually recognized as such, but is thought to be both an urban product and an urban problem: the tons of garbage and sewage that are burned or buried or flushed into rivers. This, like all waste, is the abuse of a resource. It was ecological stupidity of exactly this kind that destroyed Rome. The chemist Liebig wrote that 'the sewers of the immense metropolis engulfed in the course of centuries the prosperity of Roman peasants.' The Roman Campagna would no longer yield the means of feeding her population; these same sewers devoured the wealth of Sicily, Sardinia, and the fertile land of the Coast of Africa."[33] In the last 100 years, with the proliferation of cities, towns, and the incredible growth of urban centers, the human population has become increasingly delinquent in restoring some of the natural fertility of soils. Man has continued to flush away millions of tons of potential plant nutrients, even while he is rapidly increasing his demands for soil fertility.[34]

In both past and present methods of handling, processing, and disposing of human body waste, new agents of environmental pollution are inevitably created. Nowadays, sewage works and water purification systems engineered with single-minded pursuit of maximum public sanitation are functioning as efficiently as expected, trapping some polluting substances in one local environment and dumping new pollutants elsewhere in the socio-ecosystem. The historical experience demonstrates that the disposal problem always remains unsolved in any solution that deals with the sanitation problem alone, rather than as a component of the general equilibrium problem. Despite visible successes obtained from nonsystemic solutions to the problem, such as the triumph of cleansing the liquid sewage so efficiently that it can be used again as water, all short-term, partial solutions to the body waste problem merely beg the crucial question, "What is the most efficient (consistently useful) way to absorb the continuous flow of human body waste in the socio-ecosystem?"

Environmental pollution is essentially a process originating in the generation and accumulation of waste in local and global communities. To solve the global body waste problem in the general context of the circular flow of material processes, an inclusive method of approach is indicated. Instead of continuing the traditional programs which extend rather than eliminate secondary displacements from the circular flow, thereby promoting pollution, new answers are required. By increasing the range and utility of material processes, the new engineering system should stimulate and enlarge the overall absorption of material resources in the socio-ecosystem, i.e., facilitate the availability of displaced resources (wastes) for effective absorption. The total impact of such physical transformation on the material balance is analogous to the effect of an innovation which increases the range of production possibilities in the socio-ecosystem, with given resource endowments. Briefly stated, the socially optimal solution to the body waste problem is offered by that engineering system which is most efficient in changing potential environmental pollutants into increased material absorptions and clean environments. It is essential to the optimal solution that body waste disposal processes function literally as material reclamation processes. In spite of the visible benefits being derived from traditional solutions to the body waste disposal problems, the feeling is now widespread that the real costs of the relevant programs in money, material, and human disutilities are growing beyond tolerable limits.[36] In addition, many people now feel that the advantages of the traditional programs no longer justify the ecological disadvantages that are seriously threatening our pollution-sensitive planetary environments.

Because of this changing attitude, the pendulum of social policy will continue to swing away from the traditional toward contemporary solutions with emphasis on inclusive pragmatism typified by agricultural sanitation, as demonstrated by the examples of China, Japan, and India. In the field of applied agricultural sanitation, the examples of China,[37] Japan,[38] and India,[39] which have acquired sufficient working knowledge, innovative experience, and valuable technical information on the treatment and utilization of sewage and night soil, are highly recommended, especially to those developing countries who have neither the requisite experience nor technical proficiency necessary for development of this process. Aside from these three national sources of international assistance, it is particularly important to acknowledge the wealth of technical know-how developed by certain agencies of the United Nations,[40] such as the FAO, WHO, and IBRD, which is available to developing countries requiring expert assistance in formulating and developing fertilizer reclamation projects. In view of these bilateral and multilateral possibilities, it is reasonable to conclude that there is an enormous international bargain in increased food and agricultural production to be reaped from this project by developing countries with the expert assistance and technology transfers from the aforementioned sources.

NOTES

1. FAO, *Organic Materials as Fertilizers*; A. C. Garg et al., *Organic Manures.*

2. LA/OMA Project Report *Sludge Processing and Disposal*, USEPA and Calif. State Water Resources Control Board, Los Angeles 1977; Sim, Van der Ryn, *The Toilet Papers*, (Santa Barbara, California: Capra Press, 1978).

3. LA/OMA Project Report, op. cit.

4. See chapter 15 for more on the aerobic method.

5. K. M. Bright, *Sludge Handling and Disposal—Phase I—State of the Art*; Report for Metropolitan Sewer Board of the Twin Cities Area, Minneapolis-St. Paul, Minnesota, (1972); J. M. Wyatt and P. E. White, *Sludge Processing Transportation and Disposal/Resource Recovery: A Planning Perspective* (Washington: EPA 1975); R. Smith and R. G. Eilers, *Wastewater Treatment Plant Cost Estimating Program* (Cincinnati, Ohio: EPA, 1971).

6. LA/OMA Project Report, loc. cit., p. 38.

7. Ibid.

8. J. M. Wyatt, and P. E. White, op. cit.; R. Smith and R. G. Eilers, op. cit.; J. B. Farrell, et al., "Lime Stabilization of Primary Sludges" in *Journal of Water Pollution Control Federation*, (Jan. 1974).

9. R. Smith and R. G. Eilers, *Computer Evaluation of Sludge Handling and Disposal Costs* (Cincinnati, Ohio: EPA).

10. G. M. Fair and J. C. Geyer, *Water Supply and Waste-Water Disposal* (New York: John Wiley & Sons, Inc., 1954).

11. *Sludge and Processed Liquid Side Streams at Water Treatment Works* (EPA, Washington, D.C.: San Francisco Bay Area Municipal Wastewater Solids Management Study, Bay Area Sewage Services Agency, San Francisco, 1975).

12. LA/OMA Project Report, loc. cit., pp. 3–17.

13. Ibid., pp. 7–11.

14. Ibid.

15. K. M. Bright, *Sludge Handling and Disposal*, loc. cit.,; J. M. Wyatt and P. E. White, *Sludge Processing . . .*, loc. cit.; G. R. Grantham, *Memorandum: Cost Curves for Basin Plans*, Report for Basin Contractors, by BCAC Subcommittee III—4, Jan. 1973; R. S. Burd, *A Study of Sludge Handling and Disposal*, Report for FWPCA, Dept. of the Interior, Washington, D.C. 1968; G. M. Malborn and E. I. Titlow, "Energy and Resource Recovery from Solid Wastes" presented at the Washington Academy of Sciences Symposium, University of Maryland, Baltimore, 1975.

16. F. M. Lewis, "Fundamentals of Pyrolysis Processes for Resource Recovery and Pollution Control" Proceedings of the 68th Annual Meeting of the Air Pollution Control Association, June 1975; F. M. Lewis, "Sludge Pyrolysis for Energy Recovery and Pollution Control" presented at the Second National Conference on Municipal Sludge Management and Disposal, Anaheim, California, Aug., 1975.

17. LA/OMA Project Report, loc. cit., pp. 7–9.

18. Ibid., pp. 7–11.

19. Ibid., pp. 7–13.

20. Ibid.

21. Ibid.

22. Sim Van der Ryn, op. cit.

23. The science of agricultural sanitation presents a viable solution offering multiple benefits to the public in potentially greater food and agricultural production and, at the same time, aid the global campaign to eliminate the scourge of fecal-borne diseases. See Chapter 11 for more discussion.

24. M. Alexander, "Degradation of Natural and Synthetic Organic Compounds in Soils," *Organic Matter and Soil Fertility* (Amsterdam: North-Holland Publishing Co., 1969), pp. 511-534; J. M. Bremmer, "Role of Organic Matter in the Nitrogen Economy in Soils," *Organic Matter & Soil Fertility*, op. cit., pp. 143–193; for historical background, interested readers should see: A. I. MacKay, *Farming and Gardening in the Bible* (Emmaus, PA.: Rodale Press, 1950), pp. 203–6; F. H. King, *Farmers of Forty Centuries* (Madison, Wisc.: Democrat, 1911), pp. 193–205; H. J. Wheeler, *Manures and Fertilizers*, McMillan & Co., N.Y., 1914, pp. 10–18; also H. W. Hinton, *Fanshen* (New York: Random House, 1966); in *Fanshen* (p. 23ff) it is said that night soil was considered so valuable that agricultural laborers were required to use the privy in the landlord's fields rather than going home to defecate on their own plots. Problems arose with contamination of water with fecal bacteria and intestinal parasites.

25. A. C. Garg, et al., *Organic Manure*, loc. cit.; FAO, *Organic Material as Fertilizers*; H. W. Hinton, op cit., OEEC, *Manures and Fertilizers* (Paris: OEEC, 1954), pp. 57–77; E. M. Bodrova and Z. D. Ozohna, *Simultaneous Applications of Organic and Mineral Fertilizers* (Jerusalem: USDA, Israel Program for Scientific Translations, 1969), pp. 72–78; A. Vivian, *First Principles of Soil Fertility* (London: Kegan Paul, Treveh, Tubner & Co., Ltd., 1908), pp. 231–32; W. O. Atwater, *Result of Field Experiments with Various Fertilizers* (Washington: USDA, 1883), p. 81.

26. W. H. Corfield, *Treatment and Utilization of Sewage* (New York: Macmillan & Co., 1887), pp. 19028, 250–258; A. Wolman, "Disposal of Man's Wastes," loc. cit.; pp. 807–816; J. S. Simmons, et al., *Global Epidemiology: A Geography of Disease and Sanitation* (London: Heinneman, 1944).

27. W. H. Corfield, op. cit., chapters 2 and 3; A. Wolman, op. cit., pp. 811–812; J. C. Scott, *Health and Agriculture in China* (London: Faber & Faber), pp. 23–30.

28. F. E. Allison, *Soil Organic Matter and Its Role in Crop Production* (New York: Elsvier Scientific Publ. Co., 1973), pp. 418–427; L. Bromfield, *Malabar Farm*, (New York: Harper & Co., 1947), pp. 151, 276; P. R. Ehrlick, *Population, Resources, Environment* (San Francisco, CA., W. H. Freeman Co., 1970), pp. 185–187; D. P. Hopkins, *Chemicals, Humus and the Soil* (Brooklyn, New York.: Chemical Pub. Co., 1948), pp. 110–181; G. R. Stewart, *Not So Rich As You Think*, (Boston: Houghton Mifflin Co., 1968), pp. 49–51. However, from the standpoint of availability of organic matter for the soil, a

complementary statement would be equally valid: that the humus value of chemical fertilizers per ton is so low that it would be exhorbitantly costly for farmers to apply it to the soil.

29. F. E. Allison, *Soil Organic Matter & Its Role in Crop Production*, loc. cit., pp. 420–460; R. Bradfield, "The Role of Organic Matter in Soil Management and the Maintenance of Soil Fertility," in *Organic Matter & Soil Fertility*, loc. cit., pp. 106–127; L. Bromfield, *Malabar Farm*, loc. cit. p. 82ff; B. Commoner, *The Poverty of Power* (New York: A. Knopf Co., 1976), pp. 173–174; W. Lockeretz, et al., "A Comparison of the Production, Economic Returns and Energy Intensiveness of Corn Belt Farms that Do and Do Not Use Inorganic Fertilizers & Pesticides," CBNS-AE-4 (St. Louis: Washington Univ. Centre for the Biology of Natural Systems, July, 1975); W. Lockeretz, et al., "Economic Performance and Energy Intensiveness on Organic and Conventional Farms in the Corn Belt: A Preliminary Comparison," *American Journal of Agricultural Economics*, #59, 2 (1977); W. Lockeretz, et al., "Economic and Energy Comparisons of Crop Production on Organic and Conventional Corn Belt Farms," in *Agriculture and Energy*, Proceedings of a conference held in St. Louis, Mo. (New York: Academic Press, 1977), pp. 85–101.

30. J. Cox (1975), "The Economic Value...," loc. cit.; J. V. Krutilla and A. C. Fisher, *The Economics of Natural Environments* (Baltimore: Johns Hopkins Press, 1974), chapter 3; W. Lockeretz, "A Comparison of the Production, Economic Returns and Energy Intensiveness...," loc. cit.; W. Lockeretz, "Economic Performance...," loc. cit; W. Lockeretz, "Economic and Energy Comparison...," loc. cit.

31. D. P. Hopkins, *Chemicals, Humus and the Soil*, loc. cit., p. 90.

32. Ibid.

33. W. Berry, *A Continuous Harmony*, (New York: Harcourt, Brace, Jovanovitch).

34. D. P. Hopkins, *Chemicals, Humus and the Soil*, loc. cit., p. 95.

35. K. W. Kapp, *The Social Costs of Private Enterprise*, Shockton Books, (New York: End Impression, 1975), pp. 81–96; I. G. Simmons, *The Ecology of National Resources*, (New York: John Wiley, 1974), pp. 316–318, 347, 371–76; Anon., "Pollution: Causes, Costs, Controls," *Chemical and Engineering News* (June, 1969), pp. 32–64; J. C. Davis, *The Politics of Pollution*, (New York: Pegasus Publ., 1970).

36. For information on the Chinese experience, see FAO, *China, Recycling of Organic Wastes in Agriculture*, Soils Bulletin #40, (Rome, 1978); James C. Scott, *Health and Agriculture in China* (London: Faber & Faber); M. G. McGarry, "The Taboo Resource—The Use of Human Excreta in Chinese Agriculture," in *The Ecologist*, 1976; F. H. King, *Farmers of Forty Centuries*, loc. cit.; J. L. Buck, et al., *Food and Agriculture in Communist China* (New York: F. Praeger, 1966), pp. 134–148.

37. For information on the Japanese experience, see T. Egawa, "Utilization of Organic Materials as Fertilizers in Japan," in FAO, *Organic Materials as Fertilizers*, Soils Bulletin #27 (Rome, 1975), pp. 266–69; T. Okura, *Agricultural Development in Modern Japan* (Tokyo: Fuji Publ. Co., 1963),

chapter 19; J. I. Nakamura, *Agricultural Production in the Economic Development of Japan 1873-1922*, (Princeton, N.J.: Princeton Univ. Press, 1966), pp. 82–84.

38. For information on the Indian experience, see P. L. Jaiswal, ed, *Handbook of Manures and Fertilizers*, (New Delhi: Indian Council on Agricultural Research, 1971); A. C. Garg, et al., *Organic Manures*, Bulletin #32 (I.C.A.R. 1971); A. Howard and Y. D. Wad, *The Waste Products of Agriculture and their Utilization as Humus*, loc. cit.

39. For example, see FAO, *Organic Materials as Fertilizers*, Soils Bulletin #27, 1975; *Organic Materials and Soil Productivity*, Soils Bulletin #35, 1978; *China: Recycling of Organic Wastes in Agriculture*, Soils Bulletin #40, Rome, 1978; *Organic Recycling in Asia and the Pacific*, Soils Bulletin (in print); WHO, *Composting: Sanitary Disposal and Reclamation of organic Wastes*, 1956; *Excreta Disposal for Rural Areas and Small Communities*, 1958; "Community Water Supply and Wastewater Disposal," in WHO Chronical Vol. 30 #8, 1976; *Management of Solid Waste in Developing Countries*, (New Delhi: South-East Asia Regional Publications, 1976); *Method of Analysis of Sewage Sludge, Solid Wastes and Compost*, CH-8600, International Reference Centre for Wastes Disposal, Geneva, 1978; IBRD, "Organic Fertilizers: Problems and Potentials for Developing Countries," in *IBRD Fertilizer Study*, 1974; *Village Water Supply*, World Bank Paper, 1976; among others.

FURTHER READING

Canale, R. P., ed. *Biological Waste Treatment*. New York: Interscience Publishers, 1971.

Crocker, T. D., and Roger, A. J. *Environmental Economics*. Hinsdale, Ill.: Dryden Press, 1971.

Department of the Environment. *Pollution: Nuisance or Nemesis*. London: HMSO, 1972.

Devik, O. *Harvesting Polluted Water*. New York: Plenum Press, 1976.

Downing, P. B. *The Economics of Urban Sewage Disposal*. New York: F. A. Praeger, 1969.

Grara, S. *Urban Planning Aspects of Water Pollution Control*. New York: Columbia University Press, 1969.

Hodges, L. *Environmental Pollution*. New York: Holt, Rinehart & Winston, 1973.

Krutilla, J. V., and Fisher, A. C. *The Economics of Natural Environments*. Baltimore: Johns Hopkins Press, 1975.

Mellamby, Sir Kenneth. *The Threat of World Pollution*. London: The Lindsey Press, 1971.

Page, T. *Economics of Involuntary Transfers: A Unified Approach to Pollution and Congestion Externalities.* New York: Springer Verlag, 1973.

Patterson, W. *Estimating Costs & Manpower Requirements for Conventional Waste Treatment Facilities.* Washington, D.C.: EPA, 1971.

Singer, S. F. *Global Effects of Environmental Pollution.* Reidel; Dordreck, 1970.

Slater, J. *Sewage Treatment, Purification & Utilization.* London: Wittaker Co., 1888.

U.S. Public Health Service. *Sewage Treatment Plants: How Much do They Cost?* Washington, D. C., 1964.

8

THE ECONOMIC VALUE OF RECOVERABLE AGRONUTRIENTS

So far, economists have not paid real attention to the
Gross National Waste of countries in their concern with
the Gross National Product.*

G. Borgstrom*

The potential social benefits of converting human waste into
agronutrients may be further elaborated by comparing the
imputed economic value of agronutrients recoverable from
human waste and chemical fertilizers. Some estimates of the
physical magnitudes, material composition, and global trends
of agronutrients recoverable from body waste have been
reviewed in preceding discussions. A graphic summary of the
physical and material dimensions is presented in separate
sections of Figure 8.1 following. With this picture in mind, we
shall consider the economic aspects of institutionalized social
wastefulness when primary waste is buried, burned, or flushed
down the drain. In exploring the economic dimension of the
waste of nations, it is also necessary to keep in mind the

*Too Many: A Study of the Earth's Biological Limitations (London:
Macmillan, 1969), p. 226.

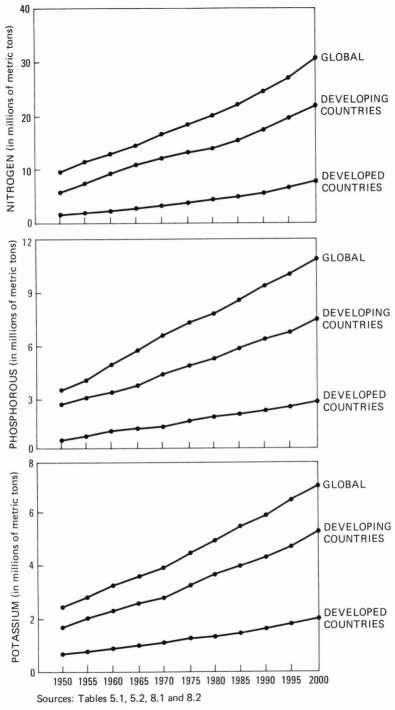

Sources: Tables 5.1, 5.2, 8.1 and 8.2

Figure 8.1 Recoverable N-P-K Nutrients from Human Waste

underlying biological processes. This understanding begins with a clear realization that the generation of primary waste is an integral component of human life processes, and that the primary waste so generated is incorporated into the circular flow of matter in socio-ecosystems.

To set the stage for an economic valuation of agronutrients recoverable from body waste, it is convenient to begin by considering the world fertilizer situation in 1975, a year when supplies were increasing and world prices were declining.[1] The declining trend began in the third quarter of 1974 after reaching a record-high level. The average world f.o.b. price for fertilizers in 1975 reflects the combined effects of the high and low monthly prices which dominated international market transactions during the first and second halves of the year.[2] The progressive decline in prices continued through the year 1975–76. The situation entered an intermediate phase in 1975 when international prices were lower than during 1974, and they continued to decline through 1976.

The equivalent money values of recoverable N, P, and K nutrients have been presented in Tables 5.1 and 5.2.[3] Beginning with Table 5.2 the total value of recoverable N, P, K nutrients in 1950 was estimated at about $6.9 billion (at 1975 world f.o.b. prices). By 1975, the aggregate value of recoverable nutrients had risen to more than $11.5 billion, about $5 billion higher than the 1950 level. The projected figures in 1975 f.o.b. world prices for 1980, 1990, and 2000 are $12.5 billion, $15.0 billion, and $18.7 billion, respectively. It may be noted, parenthetically, that from 1980 on, the projected values average out to more than $1 billion per month. These are huge sums that could be used to enrich nations as well as the earth.

A categorical two-way allocation of the potential global losses between countries in the developed and the developing worlds, presented in Tables 8.1 and 8.2, reveals some interesting contrasts. In 1950, for example, the quantity of recoverable N, P, and K nutrients originating in the developing world[4] was estimated at approximately $5 billion. By 1975, it had risen to more than $8 billion. The corresponding figures for the developed world[5] were approximately $2 billion in 1950 and

TABLE 8.1. DEVELOPED COUNTRIES: Amounts and Value[a] of Agronutrients Recoverable from Human Waste.

Amounts in Million Metric Tons

	1950	1955	1960	1965	1970	1975	1980	1985	1990	1995	2000
Humuscite (Ω)	17.50	19.00	20.50	23.00	27.00	31.00	32.50	34.00	37.50	41.50	45.50
Nitrogen (N)	2.91	3.17	3.49	3.85	4.25	5.07	5.17	5.71	6.30	6.95	7.67
Phosphorous (P)	1.19	1.30	1.43	1.58	1.74	2.08	2.12	2.34	2.58	2.85	3.15
Potassium (K)	0.76	0.81	0.89	0.99	1.09	1.30	1.32	1.46	1.61	1.78	1.97
Total: N+P+K	4.86	5.28	5.81	6.44	7.08	8.45	8.61	9.51	10.48	11.58	12.79

Value: in Billion Dollars

	1950	1955	1960	1965	1970	1975	1980	1985	1990	1995	2000
Nitrogen (N)	1.29	1.41	1.55	1.71	1.88	2.25	2.29	2.53	2.79	3.08	3.40
Phosphorous (P)	0.51	0.56	0.62	0.68	0.75	0.89	0.92	1.01	1.11	1.23	1.36
Potassium (K)	0.09	0.10	0.11	0.13	0.14	0.16	0.17	0.18	0.20	0.23	0.25
Total: N+P+K	1.90	2.02	2.28	2.52	2.77	3.31	3.38	3.73	4.11	4.54	5.01

[a] Money value is calculated at 1975 world f.o.b. prices. See Appendix A for principal sources.

TABLE 8.2. DEVELOPING COUNTRIES: Amounts and Value[a] of Agronutrients Recoverable from Human Waste.

Amounts in Million Metric Tons

	1950	1955	1960	1965	1970	1975	1980	1985	1990	1995	2000
Humuscite (Ω)	42.5	45.5	49.5	57.0	63.0	69.0	77.5	81.5	90.0	99.5	109.5
Nitrogen (N)	7.83	8.54	9.39	10.34	11.89	13.05	14.36	15.36	16.96	18.72	21.12
Phosphorous (P)	2.96	3.23	3.55	3.91	4.49	4.93	5.43	5.80	6.41	7.07	7.98
Potassium (K)	1.62	2.09	2.30	2.53	2.91	3.19	3.51	3.75	4.15	4.58	5.16
Total: N+P+K	12.41	13.86	15.24	16.78	19.29	21.17	23.30	24.91	27.52	30.37	34.26

Value: in Billion Dollars

	1950	1955	1960	1965	1970	1975	1980	1985	1990	1995	2000
Nitrogen (N)	3.47	3.79	4.16	4.58	5.27	5.78	6.37	6.81	7.52	8.30	9.36
Phosphorous (P)	1.28	1.40	1.53	1.69	1.94	2.13	2.35	2.51	2.77	2.99	3.40
Potassium (K)	0.21	0.27	0.29	0.32	0.37	0.41	0.45	0.48	0.53	0.58	0.66
Total: N+P+K	4.96	5.45	5.99	6.60	7.58	8.32	9.16	9.79	10.82	11.87	13.47

[a]Money value is calculated at 1975 world f.o.b. prices. See Appendix A for principal sources.

$3.3 billion in 1975. Between 1950 and 1975, the monetary value of the nutrients originating in the developing world was more than twice as large as that of the developed world. If the underlying trends continue, the projected figures for the developing world in 1980, 1990, and 2000 will be $9.2 billion, $10.8 billion, and $13.5 billion, respectively; the projections for the developed world, over the same period, are $3.5 billion, $4.1 billion, and $5.0 billion.

To see the composition of the global figures in greater detail, the figures for 1975 will be disaggregated in an attempt to show the regional and intraregional magnitudes, and to present as much analytical and descriptive information as possible on the economic value of N, P, and K nutrients recoverable from human waste. The total value of recoverable N, P, and K nutrients in 1975 was a little more than $11.5 billion (at 1975 world f.o.b. prices of chemical fertilizers). In Table 8.3, the geographic composition of this aggregate value is given as follows:[6] *Asia*, 17.04 million metric tons valued at more than $6.7 billion; *Europe* (including the USSR), 5.16 million metric tons valued at more than $2.0 billion; *America* (North and South), 4.03 million metric tons valued at approximately $1.6 billion; *Africa*, 2.97 million metric tons valued at approximately $1.2 billion; *Oceania*, 0.15 million metric tons valued at approximately $0.06 billion. One noticeable feature of the geographic distribution is that it is highly concentrated. Asia accounts for about 58 percent of the global total. In comparison with other geographic areas, the quantity originating in Asia is at least three, four, and five times as large as the corresponding share of Europe, America and Africa, respectively.

As a final review of the 1975 figures, the continental shares have been subdivided into key regional areas in order to examine the regional distribution patterns. A detailed listing of countries included in each of the main geographic regions is presented in Appendix B for easy reference. Highlights of the quantities summaried for each region, shown below in Tables 8.4 through 8.7 are as follows: *The position of Asia in 1975*:[7] The estimates of recoverable agronutrients for Asia, in physical and monetary values, indicate a record-high concentration at

TABLE 8.3. Amounts and Value[a] of Agronutrients Recoverable from Human Waste — By Geographic Composition – 1975.

	Amounts in million metric tons					Value in Million Dollars			
	Humus-cite (Ω)	Nitrogen (N)	Phosphorous (P)	Potassium (K)	Total N+P+K	N	P	K	Total N+P+K
World	99.10	17.97	7.03	4.35	29.36	7966.1	3044.1	552.5	11562.9
Asia	55.79	10.43	4.08	2.53	17.04	4623.6	1764.2	321.3	6709.1
Europe (including U.S.S.R.)	16.88	3.16	1.24	0.76	5.16	1400.8	536.2	96.5	2033.5
America	13.21	2.47	0.97	0.60	4.03	1095.0	419.4	76.2	1590.6
Africa	9.74	1.82	0.71	0.44	2.97	806.8	307.0	55.9	1169.7
Oceania	0.48	0.09	0.04	0.02	0.15	39.9	17.3	2.5	59.7

[a] Money value is calculated at 1975 world f.o.b. prices.
See Appendix B for an exhaustive listing of countries, and Appendix A for detailed references.

both intercontinental and intracontinental levels of distribution. The proportion of continental total originating from East Asia was approximately 47 percent, followed by Middle South Asia with 35.9 percent, Southeast Asia with 13.6 percent, and Southwest Asia with 3.6 percent. In monetary terms, these relative shares are valued at $3.1 billion, $2.4 billion, $0.9 billion, and $0.25 billion, respectively. *The position of Europe in 1975:*[8] The estimated value of N, P, and K nutrients generated in Europe (including the USSR) is at least $2.0 billion, or 17.6 percent of the global total. The proportion represented by the contribution of the USSR (34.8 percent) is the largest single regional share in continental Europe. The share of western Europe, estimated at more than $0.4 billion (or 21.1 percent) is the second largest, followed in declining order by the following; southern Europe, eastern Europe, and northern Europe with 18.4 percent, 14.5 percent, and 10.9 percent respectively. Comparing these figures with those of other major continental areas, it is interesting to note that the degree of concentration which they represent is the lowest overall. *The position of America (North and South) in 1975:*[9] The combined values of recoverable N, P, and K nutrients originating in the Americas is estimated at approximately $1.6 billion. At least 57 percent of the total (about $0.9 billion) comes from Latin America, and the remaining 43 percent is accounted for by North America, most of it from the United States. The distribution among the regions comprising the American continent was marked by comparatively high concentration. The United States figure represents 41.7 percent of the total, followed by tropical South America, 31.7 percent; middle Latin America, 13.6 percent; temperate South America, 7.2 percent; and the Caribbean, 4.9 percent. *The position of Africa in 1975:*[10] Africa's global contribution to the money value of recoverable N, P, K is approximately $1.2 billion, or roughly 10 percent of the total. The regional distribution of this aggregate, in declining proportion, is as follows: West Africa, 32.0 percent; East Africa, 27.3 percent; North Africa, 22.9 percent; Middle Africa, 11.1 percent; South Africa, 6.7 percent.

TABLE 8.4. ASIA (including Oceania): Amounts and Values of Agronutrients Recoverable from Human Waste - 1975.

	Amounts in million metric tons					Value in Million Dollars			
	Humus-cite (Ω)	Nitro-ogen (N)	Phos-phorous (P)	Potas-sium (K)	Total N+P+K	N	P	K	Total N+P+K
Asia	56.27	10.52	4.12	2.54	17.19	4663.5	1781.5	322.6	6767.6
Southwest Asia	2.05	0.38	0.15	0.09	0.63	168.5	64.9	11.4	244.8
Southeast Asia	7.56	1.42	0.55	0.34	2.31	629.5	237.8	43.2	910.5
Middle South Asia	20.07	3.75	1.47	0.91	6.13	1662.3	635.6	115.6	2413.5
East Asia	26.09	4.88	1.91	1.18	7.97	2163.3	825.9	149.9	3139.1
Oceania	0.48	0.09	0.04	0.02	0.15	39.9	17.3	2.5	59.7

aMoney value is calculated at 1975 world f.o.b. prices.
See Appendix B for an exhaustive listing of countries, and Appendix A for detailed references.

TABLE 8.5. EUROPE (including USSR): Amounts and Value[a] of Agronutrients Recoverable from Human Waste – 1975.

| | Amounts in million metric tons | | | | | Value in Million Dollars | | | |
	Humus- cite (Ω)	Nitro- ogen (N)	Phos- phorous (P)	Potas- sium (K)	Total N+P+K	N	P	K	Total N+P+K
Europe Northern	16.88	3.16	1.24	0.76	5.16	1400.8	536.2	96.5	2033.5
Europe Western	1.9	0.35	0.14	0.06	0.58	155.2	60.5	7.6	223.3
Europe Eastern	3.6	0.67	0.26	0.16	1.09	297.0	112.4	20.3	429.7
Europe Southern	2.45	0.46	0.18	0.11	0.75	203.9	77.8	14.0	295.7
Europe	3.09	0.58	0.23	0.14	0.94	257.1	99.5	17.8	374.4
USSR	5.89	1.10	0.43	0.27	1.80	487.6	185.9	34.3	707.8

[a] Money value is calculated at 1975 world f.o.b. prices.
See Appendix B for an exhaustive listing of countries, and Appendix A for detailed references.

TABLE 8.6. AMERICA (North and South): Amounts and Value[a] of Agronutrients Recoverable from Human Waste – 1975

| | Amounts in million metric tons | | | | | Value in Million Dollars | | | |
	Humus-cite (Ω)	Nitrogen (N)	Phosphorous (P)	Potassium (K)	Total N+P+K	N	P	K	Total N+P+K
Americas North	13.21	2.47	0.97	0.60	4.03	1095.0	419.4	76.2	1590.6
America Middle South	5.62	1.05	0.41	0.25	1.72	465.5	177.3	31.8	674.6
America Tropical South	1.81	0.34	0.13	0.08	0.55	150.7	56.2	10.2	217.1
America Temperate South	4.18	0.78	0.31	0.19	1.28	345.8	134.0	24.1	503.9
America	0.97	0.18	0.07	0.04	0.29	79.8	30.3	5.1	115.2
Caribbean	0.63	0.12	0.05	0.03	0.19	53.2	21.6	3.8	78.5

[a]Money value is calculated at 1975 world f.o.b. prices.
See Appendix B for an exhaustive listing of countries, and Appendix A for detailed references.

TABLE 8.7   AFRICA: Amounts and Value[a] of Agronutrients Recoverable from Human Waste – 1975

| | Amounts in million metric tons | | | | | Value in Million Dollars | | | |
	Humus-cite (Ω)	Nitro-ogen (N)	Phos-phorous (P)	Potas-sium (K)	Total N+P+K	N	P	K	Total N+P+K
Africa	9.74	1.82	0.71	0.44	3.00	806.8	307.0	55.9	1169.7
North Africa	2.25	0.42	0.16	0.10	0.69	186.2	69.2	12.7	268.1
West Africa	3.11	0.58	0.23	0.14	0.95	257.1	99.5	17.8	374.4
East Africa	2.70	0.50	0.19	0.12	0.81	221.7	82.2	15.2	319.1
Middle Africa	1.06	0.20	0.08	0.05	0.32	88.7	34.6	6.4	129.7
South Africa	0.65	0.12	0.05	0.03	0.20	53.2	21.6	3.8	78.6

[a]Money value is calculated at 1975 world f.o.b. prices
See Appendix B for an exhaustive listing of countries, and Appendix A for detailed references.

95

A word about interpreting and applying these figures. Beneath the calm statistical surface is commingled an assortment of "soft" and "hard" statistical estimates, based on varying degrees of data availability and experience. Above all, the magnitudes presented are to be taken only as rough indicators of unknown aggregates. Inferences about specific countries may not necessarily be valid without making appropriate adjustments. For one thing, the calculations are based on gross output figures or normalized values for body waste. The actual amount of body waste that could be utilized is determined by the gross output figures, with the necessary adjustments for wastages that will normally occur in the process of collection, handling, and conservation of the raw materials. Even more importantly, the production cost of agronutrients has yet to be explicitly taken into account.[11] Thirdly, as shown earlier in chapter 7, the production possibilities for converting body waste into agronutrients are numerous and include a wide variety of physical, chemical, and biological processes ranging from labor-intensive to capital-intensive techniques.[12] Consequently, the production costs are quite varied. The behavior of total cost and the relationship between the "fixed" and the "variable" components depends largely on the processing method utilized. By the very nature of the special problems posed by the management of body waste in socio-ecosystems, the choice of a socially optimal process among a variety of labor-intensive and capital-intensive techniques cannot be made on the basis of the conventional calculus of efficiency or private profitability alone, because of the presence and total effects of manifold externalities.

It may be noted that China and India are among the leading countries to experiment with and apply organic compost made from body waste and cellulose materials or refuse.[13] In both countries, the production methods tend to be labor-intensive. In India, for example, the average "price works out to approximately $1.00 per metric ton of processed urban compost."[14] It has been suggested that "the total cost of processing the Indian potential for urban compost would come to 8 million US dollars."[15] Like India, many of the developing countries, if properly motivated to do so, are apt to adopt labor-intensive techniques to recover agronutrients from body waste.[16] Even after making the appropriate adjustments for production cost at levels comparable to those prevailing in India, it would appear that the net private and social gains to be realized from converting body waste into agronutrients—based on the cost of importing equivalent amounts of N, P, and K nutrients—are indeed enormous.

NOTES

1. USDA, *Fertilizer Situation—1977*, Economic Research Service (Washington, D.C.: GPO, January, 1977), pp. 20–23.

2. UN-FAO, *Monthly Bulletin of Agricultural Economics and Statistics*, Vol. 25 (Rome: July/August 1976), pp. 16–28.

3. Principal sources of estimation are USDA, *Fertilizer Situation—1977*; UN-FAO, *Monthly Bulletin of Agricultural Economics and Statistics*; USDA, *World Fertilizer Review and Prospects to 1980/81*; UN-FAO, "Longer-Term Fertilizer Supply/Demand Position and Elements of a World Fertilizer Policy," AGS: F/75/7 (May 1975); FAO Commission on Fertilizers, 2nd Session, Rome, June 3–7, 1975; British Sulphur Corporation, *Fertilizer International* 89 (November 1976), p. 5; UN-FAO, *Organic Material as Fertilizers*, chapter 3; J. J. C. Van Voorheve, "Organic Fertilizers: Problems and Potentials for Developing Countries".

4. See Table 8.2.

5. See Table 8.1.

6. See Table 8.3.

7. See Table 8.4 and Appendix B.

8. See Table 8.5 and Appendix B.

9. See Table 8.6 and Appendix B.

10. See Table 8.7 and Appendix B.

11. M. V. Bopardikar, "Optimum Utilization of Compost in India," *Compost Science*, no. 5 (1976), pp. 22–23; A. C. Garg, et al., *Organic Manures*, loc. cit.; FAO, *Organic Material as Fertilizers*, op. cit.; J. Goldstein, *Sensible Sludge* (Emmaus, PA.: Rodale Books, 1977).

12. C. G. Golueke, *Composting*; C. G. Golueke, *Biological Reclamation of Solid Wastes* (Emmaus, PA.: Rodale Books, 1977); C. G. Golueke, "Composting: A Review of Rationale, Principles and Public Health," *Compost Science* 17 no. 3 (1976), pp. 11015; A. C. Garg, op. cit.; J. Goldstein, op. cit.; FAO *Organic Materials as Fertilizers*; FAO *Organic Materials and Soil Productivity*; Roger Blobaum, "China Recycles Her Wastes by Using Them on the Land," *Compost Science* 16 no. 5 (1975), pp. 16–17.

13. C. Y. Tang, *An Economic Study of Chinese Agriculture*, PhD. thesis, Cornell University, 1924, pp. 102–103; *Chinese Medical Journal*, 1975, loc.

cit.; A. C. Garg, op. cit.; FAO, *Organic Materials As Fertilizers;* C. Golueke, *Composting,* op. cit.; Roger Blobaum, op. cit.; M. V. Bopardiker, "Optimum Utilization of Compost in India,"; J. K. McMichael, *Health in the World,* Studies from Vietnam (Nottingham, England: Spokesman Books, 1976); J. C. Scott, op. cit.; FAO, *China.*

14. Ibid.

15. FAO, *Organic Materials as Fertilizers,* p. 22.

16. Ronald Gurak, et al., "Compost Latrines in Tanzania," *Compost Science* 18 no. 4 (1977), pp. 20–23; W. Rybczynski, *The Minimum Composting Toilet,* Report to U.N.E.P. and National Housing Authority (Manila, Philippines), 1976; J. K. McMichael, op. cit.; R. Blobaum, op. cit.; Abby Rockefeller, "Private Profit and Public Waste: The Connection," *Compost Science* 17 no. 4 (1976), pp. 13–15; Harold Leich, "New Options for a Sewerless Society," *Compost Science* 17 no. 3, pp. 7–10.

FURTHER READING

Bidlack, B., et al. *Future Food Resources—A Challenge for Today.* Claremont College, CA, 1975.

Feeding the World in the Year 2000: A Symposium, The Futurist, 1975, 9 (6).

Framingham, C. F. *The World Food Needs of the 1980's.* Dept. of Agricultural Economics and Farm Management. Manitoba, Canada: University of Manitoba, 1974.

Gifford, R. M., and Millington, R. J. *Energetics of Agricultural and Food Production,* Bulletin of Commonwealth Scientific and Industrial Research Organization, #288. Australia, 1975.

Jones, D. *Food and Interdependence.* London: UK Overseas Development Institute, 1976.

Marei, S. A. *The World Food Crisis.* London: Longman Group Ltd., 1976.

Martin, W. P., ed. *All-out Food Production: Strategy and Resource Implications.* Special Publication of the American Society for Agronomy, 1975.

OECD, *Unconventional Foodstuffs for Human Consumption.* Paris, 1975.

Steele, F., and Bourne, A., eds. *The Man/Food Equation.* New York: Academic Press, 1975.

Utrecht, E. "An Alternative Report on World Hunger" in *Cultures et Development* (1976) 8 (1).

Wagstaff, H. *World Food: A Political Task.* Fabian Research Series. #326. London: Fabian Society, 1976.

Walston, Lord. *Dealing with Hunger.* Canada: The Bodley Head, 1976.

PART IV: PROGRAMS:
The Role of Chemical Fertilizers and Body Waste Nutrients

9

FERTILIZERS IN WORLD AGRICULTURE AND FOOD PRODUCTION

The law of the immobility of the mineral elements in the soil explains the agricultural experience of the ages, . . . that no plant can be profitably cultivated upon a soil, unless the mineral contents of the soil are in proportion to the special requirements of that plant. . . . Hence, the art of the agriculturist mainly consists in selecting such plants as will thrive best in his land, . . . and in using all the means at his command to make the nutritive elements in chemical combination available for plants.

Justus von Liebig*

The use of natural fertilizers made of animal and plant wastes is a basic feature of an ages-old evolutionary process. As a special extension of this process, the application of synthetic plant foods (fertilizers made of various combinations of chemical compounds of which nitrogen, phosphorous, and potassium

*The Natural Law of Husbandry (New York: Appleton & Co., 1863), p. 129.

are the major inputs) has now become the predominant method of plant fertilization in world agriculture. Nevertheless, it is important to note that the production and utilization of such fertilizers are comparatively recent developments in the history of agriculture. A review of an ancient record on the subject reveals that Mahamuni Parasara, the author of Krishi Sangraha written in the Sanskrit language more than 3000 years ago and perhaps the oldest handbook on agriculture paid considerable attention to "how the heap of cow dung should be worshipped, reverently treated, and utilized at the sowing time."[1] On the same subject, the other authoritative sources[2] (Cato, Xenophon, Varro, Columella, in their classic works on agriculture) also paid due attention to the inestimable value of animal manure and pointed out that both the Greeks and Romans used green manure although the scientific explanation of why peas and vetches enrich the soil with their nitrogen-fixing properties was not discovered by Hellriegel and Wilfarth until 1886, more than 2000 years later.[3] For the most part, it appears that the social history of agriculture in the last few hundred years was shaped indelibly by the combined impact of autonomous and induced forces: biological necessity (i.e., rapid population expansion) on the one hand, and the ruthless push of economic self-interest (e.g., rapid exploitation of land) on the other. Operating like the familiar "carrot and stick" incentives, the dynamic effects of unrelenting pressure from both sources have driven and are driving landowners and farmers in different areas of the world to apply various fertilizing substances to the soil, according to prevailing local ideas on agriculture.

THE DEVELOPMENT OF CHEMICAL FERTILIZERS

The emergence of chemical fertilizers was facilitated in part by a complete understanding of the fundamental principles of manuring and, above all, by a rational understanding of the problems of plant nutrition as demonstrated by the pioneering works of a number of agricultural scientists, including Priestly, de Saussure, Sprengel, Bousingault and Liebig, to mention only a few.[4] A retrospective look at this development from as early as the seventeenth century shows that hundreds of years of long, painful, and laborious efforts had elapsed before the farmers, scientists, and agricultural engineers finally achieved sufficient technological breakthroughs which made possible the establishment of the modern fertilizer industry. In the long search for a solution, Dr. John Woodward of London discovered in 1669 that plant growth increased with greater sediment in water;[5] about two centuries later, in 1843 Sir John Bennet Lawes of Rotharmstead produced the first superphosphate fertilizer;[6] and from 1843 to the contemporary the late 1970s, fertilizer technology has taken such a quantum leap forward that standardized technology for manufacturing synthetic nitrogen/phosphate/potassium fertilizers is virtually a universal reality.

The nineteenth century marked the dawning of the age of synthetic chemical fertilizers. Taking the problems of environmental side effects duly into account, the long-term impact of synthetic fertilizers on agriculture and animal husbandry has been generally positive and, sometimes, revolutionary in increasing the yield of plants and animals in different parts of the world. It is undoubtedly a remarkable industrial accomplishment that the first superphosphate manufactured by Sir John Bennet Lawes more than 135 years ago has opened up such expansionary waves of opportunities for farmers and industrialists; that venture marked the beginning of an era of new material development and industrial progress which created a wide variety of substitute and complementary agricultural inputs including nitrate and potash fertilizers. A brief sketch of the development of the new fertilizers during the nineteenth century, including some of the influential factors behind their different phases of evolution, is presented in the following sections.

THE EMERGENCE OF NITROGENEOUS FERTILIZER

Nitrogen is generally regarded as the premier substance among the major elements of plant nutrition. In effect, nitric acid compounds have been known and used in a variety of ways for a long time. It may be noted, for example, that the term "salt petre" which originated and was used in the twelfth century to designate nitrate of potash is still in popular use today. Although nitrate of potash itself forms an excellent artificial fertilizer, the compound was too expensive in the early period to meet agricultural requirements. For several centuries before 1800, the geographic sources and availability of salt petre (India, Hungary, Spain) supplied barely enough to meet the combined needs of industry and agriculture in Europe. Consequently, there was constant scarcity of this commodity in international commerce until the "discovery of an important deposit of nitrate of soda in [South] America, the working of which was commenced in the years 1825–1828, enabled the wants of agricluture to be met."[7] In subsequent years, nitrate of soda became the most widely known and utilized of all nitrate fertilizers. The special value of nitrate of soda as a fertilizer lies in its immediate availability and direct effect on vegetative growth. As early as 1830, large quantities of nitrate of soda were being exported to Europe from the deposits in Chile. In the succeeding decades, shipments increased rapidly to about 5 million tons. As a testimony to its vast agricultural importance, the exports from Chile alone between 1907 and 1908 were estimated at more than two million tons.[8] In addition to nitrate of soda, there are two other broad categories of nitrogenous fertilizers: composted plant and animal wastes, and synthetically combined atmospheric nitrogen. The types of nitrogen fertilizers available from these three sources are not only qualitatively differentiated by their chemical composition, but also by their mode of action (slow- versus fast-acting varieties) in the soil.

THE EMERGENCE OF PHOSPHATIC FERTILIZERS

The superphosphate fertilizer industry was one of the earliest practical consequences of Liebig's mineral manure theory published in 1840.[9] In 1842 Sir John Bennet Lawes, the first manufacturer of phosphatic fertilizer, took out his patent on superphosphate.[10] The essential task in the manufacture of superphosphate is to convert raw phosphates containing phosphoric acid by treating them with sulphuric acid. The product so converted is readily absorbed and assimilated by plants. Despite the efficacy of the new innovation, the use of mineral phosphates as fertilizer was quantitatively insignificant during the five years after Sir John Bennet Lawes acquired his patent. Production and utilization of superphosphates expanded enormously, however, after coprolytes were discovered in England, at the beginning of the second half of the nineteenth century. The industry spready to Germany, France, and other countries in Europe which had ample supplies of the basic raw material. The most common phosphates found in artificial fertilizers are the phosphates of lime which, unlike the limited geographic occurrence of nitrates and potash, are found in geologic deposits over the globe and have been commercially exploited for a long time in various countries. In the last decades of the nineteenth century, large quantities of the deposits excavated in France, Belgium, Russia, and Africa were being used by the phosphatic fertilizer industry to meet the rapidly expanding requirements of modern agriculture.

THE EMERGENCE OF POTASSIC FERTILIZER

Long before the creation of the modern potash industry, the fertilizing value of wood ashes had been known by the ancients who employed it in farming and industry. But as long as wood ashes remained the primary source of potash, the salts of potash could not be obtained in quantities or at prices appropriate to growing agricultural requirements. The manufacture and distribution of potassic fertilizers on a large scale did not begin until the development of the Strassfurt potash deposits in Germany during the 1860s. The technical judgment of geologists and chemical engineers engaged in this venture was that, in addition to other valuable minerals present in the deposits, the qualitative significance of potassium and especially magnesium chloride contained in the Strassfurt salts render them highly practical, if not industrially ideal, for making synthetic chemical fertilizer. Supported by rich and abundant resource endowments, the success of the potassic fertilizer industry was immediate and so substantial that "by 1900 no less than 1,158,000 tons of potash salts from Strassfurt were being used for agricultural purposes alone."[11] Thanks largely to her decisive resource advantage and policy of rapid consolidation and expansion of her potash industry throughout the second half of the nineteenth century, Germany emerged as the dominant world producer, processor, and distributor of potassium fertilizer on the eve of World War I.

Viewed from the organization approach, the world fertilizer industry is comprised of all producers, processors, and distributors of the three principal plant nutrients: the nitrogeneous, phosphatic, and potassic fertilizers. In the early period of the industry's development, the geographic network of industrial activity was well established in Europe, and to some extent in America. By consolidating their strategic locational and technological advantages, the dominant position of certain fertilizer-producing countries remained virtually unchallenged well into the twentieth century. On the eve of World War I, and to a large extent throughout the interwar years, the German potash cartel and the Chilean nitrate syndicate dominated the international markets for two of the three strategic fertilizer raw materials. (The United States, French North Africa, and Russia were the most influential suppliers of phosphate rocks.) In contrast to the prewar era, the geographic pattern of post-World War II activity in the fertilizer industry (producers, processors, and distributors) appears on the surface to be more widely diffused, and the global concentration of industrial ownership, material control, production and consumption of nitrogen-phosphate-potassium nutrients is now increasing faster than at any other period since the latter part of the nineteenth century.

The question of crop yields is a necessary extension of the foregoing discussion. In aggregate terms, what is the net impact of chemical fertilizer production, consumption, and trade on world agriculture and food production? A complete analysis of this question would require detailed information on fertilizer application in every country, particularly in the nineteenth century. However, a concise statement for a corresponding period of time will suffice for our immediate purposes. In stark contrast to the 10-bushel yields common in feudal times, the application of chemical fertilizers has brought modern agriculture to a stage where "yields of 40 to 50 bushes of wheat per acre are fairly common, and yields of near 100 bushels have been achieved."[12] In physical terms, this scale of transformation is equivalent in magnitude to an average increase in productivity of between 400 and 500 percent and, in extreme cases, as high as 1,000 percent of the prevailing standards of the early period.

The post-World War II global expansion in agricultural production was truly revolutionary. Perhaps the most important feature of this development was that agricultural production achieved an unprecendented scale of productivity without significant expansion of the total land under cultivation.[13] For example, more than 70 percent of the change in total output in cereal grains was due to intensive land utilization aided by extraintensive fertilizer consumption per hectare. In particular, the increase in fertilizer intensity per hectare in developed countries—on the average, about five-fold—was quite unprecedented in the long history of world agriculture.[14] Indeed, it may be said that next to sweet water, fertilizers are truly the elixirs of terrestrial agricultural life. It is crucial, in this connection, to understand and appreciate the decisive role fertilizers play in the evolution of world agriculture and food production and, ultimately, in the changing character of human life on earth in its biological, physical, and social manifestations.[15]

Following the processes developed by Lawes and others, today's synthetic chemical fertilizers are obtained from the three elements most important in plant nutrition: nitrogen, phosphorous, and potassium. Billions of dollars have been invested in these processes, and resources estimated in hundreds of millions of dollars are currently committed by private and public institutions all over the world in support of the fertilizer industry.[16] The methods of Liebig and Lawes have continued to dominate the industry, if not the content of research and development in the "synthetic" (that is, the inorganic) as opposed to the "natural" (organic) chemical fertilizers.[17] It has been alleged that the historical dominance of the synthetic method probably hindered a balanced development and the evolution of unfettered research for other solutions, such as in the field of humus and related natural plant nutrients.[18] The controversies over this have polarized the experts into two feuding camps, the "Organic School" and the "Inorganic School." The obfuscating fall-out from the fanatics of both sides has generated more heat than light, but the debate may yet contribute significant solutions to some of the major problems of agriculture and world food supply. If the prevailing philosophical and methodological conflicts between the extreme members of the two schools should continue unresolved, it might hamper an early integration of constructive technical efforts. Yet it is commonly agreed that, more than any other factor, the cooperative effort of the whole community of scientists in the field of agriculture is necessary if optimal solutions are to be found.

POSTWAR CONSUMPTION OF SYNTHETIC CHEMICAL FERTILIZERS

In 1950, the total world consumption of fertilizers was approximately 14.0 million metric tons.[19] Ten years later, it had risen to 28.5 million metric tons—more than twice the level established in 1950. By 1970, global consumption had reached 68 million metric tons. At the current rate of growth, it is estimated that aggregate consumption will probably rise to about 120 million metric tons in 1980. According to these figures, the net change in global consumption between 1950 and 1975 is about 80 million metric tons, which represents an increase of more than 600 percent in 25 years. The trend observed in world commercial fertilizer consumption was also reflected in per capita consumption figures: 5.5 kilograms in 1950; 9.6 kilograms in 1960; 19.0 kilograms in 1970, and 23.0 kilograms in 1975. Global fertilizer consumption per hectare was 9.2 kilograms in 1950; 19.0 in 1960; 45.5 in 1970; and 60.0 kilograms in 1975.[20] On the whole, the figures indicate that the volume of fertilizer consumption per hectare was at least twice as large as the corresponding figures per capita.

How helpful is this statistical information for understanding future developments? First, the descriptive significance of the data being presented rests, in part, on the intertemporal connection between present and future movements in aggregate demand for fertilizers. Secondly, a large number of countries, if not all, provide varying degrees of information on commercial fertilizer consumption per capita as well as per hectare. Much can be learned about the underlying behavior of the global aggregates by evaluating the correlation between their mean values and the corresponding individual country data. In 1975, for example, the mean values of global fertilizer consumption were 20.6 kilograms per capita and 52.4 kilograms per hectare respectively. The corresponding figures for individual countries varied roughly between one and 173 kilograms per capita, and between one and 602 kilograms per hectare. The indicated range of deviation between the global average and the individual country per capita consumption data is—roughly—10 kilograms to 153 kilgrams. This magnitude is large, even by world standards. It shows, among other things, that the distribution of per capita consumption figures among individual countries is extremely skewed. With regard to the mean values for consumption per hectare, the same observation is valid, though the range of deviation between the global and individual countries is even wider: 51 kilograms to 550 kilograms. The data for 1975 also confirm the same tendency towards increased concentration of commercial fertilizer consumption, and the implied worsening of the distribution of global fertilizer output between the competing needs of developed and developing countries.

The systemic link between the world demand for fertilizers and the crisis in world food supply is established directly through the positive impact of fertilizers on the productive efficiency of world's agricultural activity. To a great extent, the prevailing global trend of the consumption of commercial fertilizers was initiated and sustained by secular changes in demand for food and other agricultural products. In aggregate volume, this global demand has expanded enormously in the last 25 years, under the combined stimulus of superaffluence in the West, improved quality of life in the Southern hemisphere, and the expanding world population. The farmers of the world have responded to increased demand by expanding the productive capacity of world agriculture throughout the postwar era. Despite the timely response of the farmers, however, the overall rate of expansion has not been fast enough, nor has the geographic distribution of new production capacity been widespread enough, to keep up with the demand. As indicated elsewhere,[21] the global record of performance in food production during the fifties and sixties was quite impressive, but it required about two-thirds of the population in developing countries, contrasted to one-fifth in the developed countries, to keep food supplies from lagging even further behind population growth. For example, the world output of cereal grains more than doubled between 1950 and 1972, while per capita output rose about 40 percent. Over the same period of time, world population increased from about 2.5 billion to 3.7 billion, approximately 50 percent. However, in spite of the long-term rise in per capita production, there was no real improvement in the global distribution of food grains. For the world as a whole, approximately equal shares of supplies went to 30 and 70 percent of world population in developed and developing countries, respectively. The world food crisis is due in part to the disproportionate per capita ration of food available to the North and South, revealing the grossly inadequate share of global food grains going to the populations of developing countries—those 3 billion or more people inhabiting Africa, Asia, and Latin America.[22] In such circumstances, malnutrition in these parts of the world is inevitable.

NOTES

1. KRISHI SANGRAHA, trans. by S. P. Chandhuri, Imperial Bureau of Soil Science *Monthly Bulletin* 59, (England, 1926); see also KRSI-PARA-SARA, ed. and trans. by S. C. Banerji, and G. P. Majumdar in *Bibliotecha Indica*, Vol. 285, 1960.

2. See Xenophon's *Oeconomicus;* Cato's *De agri cultura;* Varro's *De re rustica;* and Columella's *De re rustica.*

3. A. D. Hall, *Fertilizers and Manures* (New York: Macmillan & Co. 1914), pp. 11 and 28; F. E. Allison, *Soil Organic Matter and Its Role in Crop Production* (London: Elsevier Scientific Publ. Co., 1973), p. 20.

4. J. von Liebig, Baron, *Letters on Modern Agriculture*, John Blyth, ed. (London: Walton and Maberly, 1854).

5. Thomas Thomson, *History of the Royal Society* (London, 1812), p. 58; see also *Philosophical Transactions*, Vol. 21 (1699), p. 193; and Henry Hallam, *Literature of Europe* (London: John Murray, 1874), Vol. III, p. 592.

6. *The Book of Rotharmstead Experiments* (London: John Murray, 1905), pp. xxii–xxiii; Mirko, Lamer, *The World Fertilizer Economy*, loc. cit., p. 37.

7. J. Fritsch, *The Manufacture of Chemical Fertilizers* (London: Scott, Greenwood & Sons, 1911), p. 219

8. Ibid., p. 223.

9. J. von Liebig, Baron, *Organic Chemistry in its Applications to Agriculture and Physiology*, Lyon Taylor and Walton, eds. (London, 1840); also *The Natural Law of Husbandry* (New York: D. Appleton & co., 1863).

10. *The Book of Rotharmstead Experiments*, op. cit., pp. xxii-xxiii; F. E. Allison, *Soil Organic Matter . . .* , loc. cit., p. 20.

11. A. D. Hall, *Fertilizer and Manures*, loc. cit., p. 159.

12. F. E. Allison, op. cit., p. 20.

13. G. Borgstrom, *The Food and People Dilemma*, loc. cit., pp. 29–45; Buringh, H. van Heemst and G. Staring, *The Absolute Maximum Food Production of the World* (Amsterdam: Wagenigen Agricultural University, 1975); FAO, *State of Food and Agriculture*, Rome Annual Publication: 1950–1975, see section on agricultural production; R. Reville, "Food and Population," *Scientific American*, loc. cit.

14. A. N. Duckham, and G. B. Masefield, *Farming Systems of the World* (London: Chatto & Windus, 1970); FAO, *Annual Fertilizer Review*, Rome, for the period 1950–1975; Proceeding of the Fertilizer Society, *Fertilizers in Retrospect and Prospect*, loc. cit.; J. Ruthenberg , "The Economics of Introducing Fertilizer," Proceedings of the 7th Colloquium of the International Potash Institute, Berne, 1969.

15. For historical survey, see G. E. Fussell, *Farming Techniques from Prehistoric to Modern Times* (New York: Pergamon, 1966); W. C. Lowdermilk, *Conquest of the Land Through 7000 Years*, U.S.D.A. Information Bulletin 99 (1953); R. Tannahill, *Food in History* (New York: Stein & Day, 1973); G. W. Cooke, *Fertilizer and Society*, loc. cit.

16. Anon., "Fertilizer Need Large Capital Investments," *Chemical Age*, London 109 (Sept. 26, 1974); Anon., "Feast and Famine—Fertilizers," *Forbes* (March 1974), 113(5); "Fertilizer Shortages Growing," *Chemical Week*, 114(7) 15 (February 13, 1974).

17. See Justus von Liebig, *The Natural Laws of Husbandry* (New York: D. Appleton, 1863)), pp. 73–1344; Sir Albert Howard, *Agricultural Testament* (Oxford Univ. Press, 1940), pp. 1–32.

18. A. Schatz, "Humus Research-East and West," *Compost Science* (Autumn 1966), pp. 19020; H. Martin-Leake, "The Resurgence of Humus," *Compost Science* (winter 1967), pp. 26–28.

19. See Table 5.3.

20. Ibid.

21. See Chapter 2; also FAO, *State of Food and Agriculture*, op. cit.; R. Reville, op. cit.

22. FAO/DD2/75/2 (1975), op. cit., pp. 40–44; J. D. Tydings, *Born to Starve*, op. cit., pp. 19–96; McNamara, R., *One Hundred Countries, Two Billion People . . .*, op. cit., pp. 29–48.

FURTHER READING

Cooke, G. W. *Fertilizing for Maximum Yield.* New York: Hefner, 1972.

Couston, J. W. *Making Fertilizer Available to Farmers.* Rome: FAO, 1963.

FAO. *Fertilizers and Their Uses.* Rome, 1970.

———. *FAO Fertilizer Program*. The First Decade. Zurich: Centre d'Étude de L'Azote, 1974.

———. *First 15 Years of the FAO Fertilizer Program 1960–75*. Rome: FAO Land & Water, 1976.

Gues, J. G. *Fertilizer Guide for the Tropics and Subtropics*, 2nd ed. Zurich: Centre d'Étude de L'Azote, 1973.

Jacob, Arthur. *Fertilizer Use: Nutrition and Manuring of Tropical Crops*. Hanover, 1960.

Linneman, H., et. al. *MOIRA: Model of International Relationsin Agriculture*. Amsterdam: North Holland Publ. Co., 1976.

McNeil, J. M. *Fertilizer Use and Crop Yields*. Washington, D. C., 1946.

Nicol, H. *Plant Growth Substances*. London: L. Hill, 1938.

Parker, F. W. *Fertilizer and Economic Development*. Rome: FAO, 1962.

Proceedings of the Fertilizer Society: *Fertilizer and Animal Productions in 1968; Nitrogen Fixation-Future Prospect 1976; The Role of World Bank in Helping to Meet the Fertilizer Requirements of Developing Countries 1976*, London.

Rutherberg, H. *Farming Systems in the Tropics*. Oxford: Clarendon Press, 1971.

Schiffelen, A. C. *Energy Balance in the Use of Fertilizers*. (Spanish) Vol. 18 no. 1, 1975.

Slack, A. V. *Defense Against Famine: The Role of Fertilizer Industry*. New York: Doubleday, 1970.

Wahhab, Abdul. "Fertilizer Trials in Farmer's Fields," Dept. of Agriculture, Govt. of West Pakistan. Lahore, 1965.

10

THE SOCIO-ECOLOGICAL EFFECTS OF CHEMICAL FERTILIZERS

A developed Agriculture is a fabulous polluter;
As development gets faster, then the problem gets
   acuter.
We are loading up the planet with a lot of nitric trash,
And if nitrogen falls off its cycle—WOW! is that a crash.

                                                    K. E. Boulding*

Man has struggled through the ages to maintain and increase the carrying capacity of arable land. Land productivity has been a crucial factor in the outcome of the global race between the growth of human population and world food supply. In modern times, the use of fertilizers has contributed to increased productivity of arable land and to the expansion of the food supply. Because of his sheer numbers and the enormous pressure he exerts on the food and agricultural resources of the earth, man occupies a crucial position in determining whether or not the balance of the natural process will be preserved. In agriculture, for example, although the stock of applicable

*"A Ballad of Ecological Awareness," in *The Careless Technology*, M. T. Farvar, ed. (New York: Natural History Press, 1972).

knowledge in agricultural chemistry and engineering has been socially beneficial, the total effects of man's role in the natural process are often unpredictable. There is a rising current of legitimate concern in many parts of the world that the impressive performance of chemical fertilizers in ensuring optimal cropping of soils is not without toxic blemishes, some of which may threaten the human ecological environments.[1]

Extensive field and research evidence has proved that compounds of phosphorous and nitrogen originating in chemical fertilizers enter the natural sources of water supply through agricultural run-off and drainage water.[2] The growing concern over concentrations of phosphorous and nitrate in community waters is due to their roles as threats to human health in methemoglobinemia, eutrophication, and depreciation of aquatic amenity. *Methemoglobinemia* is linked to excessive levels of nitrate in surface and subsurface waters. The danger to human beings arises from the fact that *nitrates* can be converted into *nitrites* by certain bacteria normally present in the digestive tract.[3] Toxicological studies have described conditions in which nitrites react with hemoglobin, forming methemoglobin which will not take up (absorb) oxygen.[4] Infants and ruminant livestock are particularly susceptible to well water containing nitrate. Nitrate is converted into nitrite in the digestive tracts of both, causing illness and sometimes death, which in infants is called methemoglobinemia (popularly known as blue baby). A significant number of deaths from the incidence of methemoglobinemia have been reported in the United States,[5] and in most of the European countries.[6]

The *eutrophication* process is characterized by an excessive enrichment of waters with nutrients,[7] and the effects include excessive growth of algae and other plant life, depletion of dissolved oxygen which promotes anaerobic bacterial action and fish kills, physical and chemical complications of water treatment problems, and a general depreciation of the amenity of aquatic resources. Among other nutrients implicated in this process, nitrogen and phosphorous have received the greatest attention because (next to carbon) they are required in substantial amounts for production of green plants. Although sewage and urban drainage provide the greatest percentages of nitrogen and phosphorous in polluted waters and nutrient run-off, agriculture also makes major contributions to the chemical discharge. The effects of eutrophication are the same whether it occurs naturally over time or is accelerated by human activities. The economic costs alone of controlling eutrophication by diversion and removal of waste water of phosphorous and nitrogen have risen to staggering proportions in recent yeas.[8] In addition to the side effects already mentioned, depreciation of aquatic amenity has become a common public concern. Aquatic resources are gifts of nature not reproducible by man, and the demand for these resources is essentially heterogeneous. Rivers and lakes are used in a variety of ways for recreation, drinking, fishing, navigation, transportation, irrigation, etc., and some of these uses may sometimes be in conflict with each other. The occurrence of water pollution which limited any of the aforementioned services would significantly depreciate the social value of aquatic amenity. A number of substances, including run-off from chemical fertilizers, can cause foul tastes and odors in waters[9] which, in turn, may render fish inedible and/or water undrinkable.[10]

Next to water, *soil pollution* has become a serious environmental threat. Although the use of chemical fertilizers has kept food production ahead of population, it has also kept soil pollution above natural levels. Among the major sources of soil pollution, inorganic salts and minerals (including the residuals of chemical fertilizers) which flow from irrigated areas are probably the most damaging to soils and plants. Salinity also aggravates the chemical imbalance of soils, impairs the delicate resiliency of natural quality, and poses a special problem in irrigation agriculture. On the whole, chemical fertilizers are, at best, nothing but expensive nuggets of mixed blessings. They contain a number of compounds relatively harmless to the soil, such as calcium, potassium, and nitrogen, as well as a long list of trace elements. Some of the trace

elements in phosphates (like arsenic, nickel, lead, tin, ur-
anium, selenium, cadmium, and tungsten) are not harmless to
man over the long term even if they enter the foodstuffs in large
quantities,[11] via the soil.

With due allowances for the contribution of other resources
to the productivity of postwar agriculture, it remains true that
the scale of intensive cultivation has been realized largely by
saturating the soil with chemical fertilizers. Although chemical fertilizers have made it possible to obtain multiple yields
impossible before the last two decades, they have often become
a serious source of pollution of both ground and surface waters.
It is further alleged that intensive soil treatment with chemical
fertilizers might have accelerated, if not created, serious health
and ecological problems by contributing directly and indirectly to environmental degradation.[12] There is evidence that
points to nutrient losses from nitrogen and phosphate fertilizers used in concentrations that transform them into eutrophic
and toxic agents. High concentrations of plant nutrients in
ground and/or surface waters, due to massive applications of
fertilizers, become serious pollutants—often damaging the
amenity of waters, accelerating algal bloom, and threatening
human life.[13] In addition to such familiar examples of the
negative impacts of chemical fertilizers, a danger to the ozone
layer from the use of phosphate fertilizers has been recently
proclaimed.[14]

The unfavorable consequences of eutrophication in the
socio-ecosystem are already well established. In addition to the
financial costs of combating pollution,[15] the rising concentration of nitrate in the community water system which may
threaten human life is frightening.[16] Despite the enormous
volume of research on this issue, the identification of nitrate
sources in water supplies remains ambiguous and contro-
versial.[17] Nevertheless, the incidence of methemoglobinemia
has been reported in a number of communities with high-
intensity application of chemical fertilizers, especially synthetic nitrogen.[18] It must be noted that the presence of nitrate in
the human body is not necessarily harmful. When specific

types of bacteria are present in the digestive tract, however, nitrate can be converted into nitrite, which is toxic. As earlier indicated, by combining with hemoglobin in the blood, it produces methemoglobinemia, a pathological manifestation which prevents the transport of oxygen by the blood. Victims of methemoglobinemia suffer from labored breathing which may end in suffocation and death. In view of present indications that certain levels of concentration of nutrient losses from chemical fertilizers are eutrophic and toxic agents, the debate is no longer whether chemical fertilizers contribute to contamination of natural waters, but what to do when the concentration of fertilizers is serious enough to warrant appropriate precautionary countermeasures.[19]

NOTES

1. E. P. Gentzch, et al, "Nitrate Occurrence in Some Soils with and without Nitric Horizons," in *Journal of Environmental Quality* 3 no. 1 (January–March, 1974), 89–94. J. I. Rodale, *Organic Gardening* (New York: Hanover House, 1955), pp. 141–150; "Nitrates: Boon or Bane," *Chemical Engineering* 76 no. 8 (1969); "Fertilizer Pollution Regulations," *Chemical Marketing Reporter* 205 no. 14 (April 1974); 14; F. G. Viets, "The Environmental Impact of Fertilizers," in CRC *Critical Review of Environmental Control* 5 no. 4, (1975) pp. 423–453; National Academy of Science, *Accumulation of Nitrates* (Washington, D. C., 1972), pp. 30–45; A. H. Walters, "Nitrates in Water, Soil, Plant, and Animals," *International Journal of Environmental Studies* 5, (1973), pp. 105–115; M. J. Romkens, and D. W. Nelson, "Phosphorous Relationships in Run Off from Fertilized Soils," *Journal of Environmental Quality* 3 no. 1 (January–March, 1974); pp. 10–12; T. Nataranger, and P. C. Sharma, "Environmental Pollution by the Phosphate Fertilizer Industry," in Proc. of the Seminar on Pollution and Human Environment (Bombay: Trombay, August, 1970), pp. 466–486.

2. For example see Department of Interior, Fed. Water Quality Admin., *Collected Papers Regarding Nitrates in Agricultural Waste Water* (Washington, D.C., 1969; USDA, *Control of Water Pollution from Cropland* vol. i (Washington, D. C., 1975); USDA, *Fate of DDT and Nitrate in Ground Water* (Washington, D.C., 1968); M. A. Bernade, *Our Precarious Habitat* (New York: W. W. Norton, 1970), chapter 8; D. Zqick and M. Benstock, *Water Wasteland* (New York: Grossman Publ., 1971), pp. 99–106; American Chemical Society, *Cleaning our Environment* (Washington, D.C.: 1969), pp. 142–144; J. Tourbier et al., *Biological Control of Water Pollution* (Philadelphia: University of Pennsylvania Press, 1976); D. Cardon, *Removal of*

Nitrate from Agricultural Tile Drainage by a Symbiotic Process (Washington; USDI, 1976).

3. R. Smith, "Significance of Methemoglobinemia in Toxicology" in *Essays in Toxicology* (New York: Academic Press, 1969), chapter 3; R. Smith, "The Nitrite-Methemoglobin Complex—Its Significance in Methemoglobin Analyses and Its Possible Role in Methemoglobinemia" in *Biochemical Pharmacology* 16, (1967), pp. 1655–1664; S. R. Tannenbaum et al., "Nitrite and Nitrate Are Formed by Endogenous Synthesis in the Human Intestine," *Science* vol. 200 (June 1978): 1487–1480; for a presentation of the chemistry of nitrosation see S. S. Marvish, in *Toxicological Applied Pharmacol.* 31, (1975), p. 325.

4. R. Smith, 1969, op. cit.; R. Smith, 1967, op. cit.; S. R. Tannenbaum, op. cit.; also S. S. Marvish, op. cit.

5. American Chemical Society, *Cleaning Our Environment*, A Report of American Chemical Soceity (Washington, D.C.: 1969), p. 143; Barry Commoner, *Closing Circle*, pp. 92–93.

6. OECD, *Impact of Fertilizer and Agricultural Waste Products on the Quality of Water* (Paris 1973), pp. 1–8; Barry Commoner, op. cit., p. 93.

7. G. A. Rohlich and K. M. Stewart, *Eutrophication—A Review*, a report submitted to the State Water Qualty Control Board (California, 1967); A. W. Taylor, "Phosphorous and Water Pollution," *Journal of Soil and Water Conservation* (November–December 1967), pp. 228–231; G. A. Rohlich, "Eutrophication" in *Municipal Sewage Effluent for Irrigation*, K. W. Wilson and F. E. Beckett, eds. (Ruston, LA: Louisiana Polytechnic Institute, 1968), pp. 159–169.

8. R. E. Train, "The Environment Today," *Science*, vol. 201 (July 18, 1978): 320–324; J. B. Karr and I. J. Schlossen, "Water Resources and the Land-Water Interface," *Science* vol. 201 (July 21, 1978): 229–234; P. R. Ehrlick, and A. H. Ehrlick, *Population, Resources, and Environment* (San Francisco: W. H. Freeman & Co., 1970), pp. 186–188; I. G. Simmons, *The Ecology of Natural Resources*, (New York: John Wiley & Sons, 1974), pp. 15, 297–299, 344–346; M. A. Bernade, op. cit., chapter 8; American Chemical Society, *Cleaning Our Environment*, pp. 142–144.

9. N. N. Gerber, and H. A. Lechevalier, "Geosmin—An Earthy-Smelling Substance Isolated from Actinomycetes," *Applied Microbiology* 13 (1965); D. E. Henley, et al., "Isolation and Identification of an Odor Compound Produced by A Selected Aquatic Actinomycetes," *Environmental Science and Technology* 3 (1969); R. S. Safferman, et al., "Earthy-Smelling Substances from A Blue-Green Alga," *Environmental Science and Technology* 1, (1967); L. L. Medsker, et al., "Odorous Compounds in Natural Waters. An Earthy-Smelling Compound Associated with Blue-Green Algae and Actinomycetes," *Environmental Science and Technology* 2 (1968).

10. J. Boetius, "Foul Taste of Fish and Oysters Caused by Chlorophenol," Medd Denmarks Fishlog Havundersdg N.S.I., 1, (1954); also see Gerber and Lechevalier, op. cit.; D. E. Henley, et al., op. cit.; R. S. Safferman, et al., op. cit.; and L. L. Medsker, et al., op. cit.

11. H. A. Schroeder, *Pollution, Profits, and Progress* (Brattleboro, Vt.: The Stephen Green Press, pp. 49–51; Barry Commoner, op. cit., p. 226; J. McHale,

World Facts and Trends, pp. 14–18; J. McHale, *The Ecological Context*, p. 12.

12. Barry Commoner, op. cit., pp. 81–93; Kettering Foundation, *The Analysis of Fertilizer Impact in the Ozone Layer*, Environmental Research and Technical Report (Dayton, Ohio, 1976); F. G. Viets, op. cit.

13. W. B. Clapham, Jr., *Natural Ecosystems* (New York: Macmillan & Co., 1973), pp. 163–166; I. G. Simmons, op. cit., pp. 297–299.

14. Kettering Foundation, *The Analysis of Fertilizer Impact in the Ozone Layer*, op. cit.

15. M. S. Commons, et al., "The Economics of Pollution and Control," *Biologist* 22(1), pp. 5–13; John A. Busterud, "The Economic Impact of Environmental Regulations," Hearings Before the Joint Economic Committee, 93rd Congress, 2nd Session, Nov. 19, 21 & 22, 1974, p. 130; J. Cox, "The Economic Value of Organic Matter in Crop Production," *Compost Science* 16(5): 24–25.

16. I. T. F. Higgins, "Importance of Epidemiological Studies Relating to Hazards of Food and Environment," *British Medical Bulletin* 31(3): 230–235, 1975.

17. M. Fried, et al., "Simplified Long Term Concept for Evaluating Leaching of Nitrogen from Agricultural Land," *Journal of Environmental Quality* 5(2): 197–200, 1976.

18. A. F. Lenain, op. cit.,; B. Commoner, op. cit.

19. Fertilizer Pollution Regulation (EPA) in *Chemical Marketing Reporter*, op. cit.

FURTHER READING

Ashton, M. D. *The Relationship of Agriculture to Soil and Water Pollution.* Report on the 1970 Cornell Agricultural Waste Management Conference. Washington, D.C., 1970.

Barut, R. F. "Environmental Protection in Sulphuric Acid, Phosphoric Acid and Complex Fertilizer Production." ISMA Technical Conference Paper 21. New York: Seville, 1972.

Bookchin, M. *Our Synthetic Environment.* (revised) New York: Harper Collophan Books, 1974.

Carson, R. *Silent Spring.* Boston: Houghton Mifflin, 1963.

Edwards, G. A. *Persistent Pesticides in the Environment.* CRC Monoscience Series. London: Buttersworth, 1970.

Fullam, H. T., & Faulkner, B. P. "Inorganic Fertilizer and Phosphate Mining Industries—Water Pollution and Control." EPA Report no. 12020, FPD 09/71. Washington, D.C.: GPO.

Hodges, L. *Environmental Pollution.* New York: Holt, Rhinehart & Winston, 1973.

King, F.C. *Gardening with Compost.* London: Faber & Faber, 1944.

Lucas, J. *Our Polluted Food.* London and New York: John Wiley & Sons, 1974.

Mishan, E. J. *The Costs of Economic Growth.* London: Stapler Press, 1967.

Proceedings of the Fertilizer Society. *Symposium on Fertilizers & The Environment,* 1976; *Some Effects of Fertilizer on Food Quality and Flavor,* 1974.

Royal Commission on Environmental Pollution. *Third Report.* HMSO, 1972.

Taylor, T. B., & Hompstone, C., *Restoration of the Earth.* New York: Harper & Row, 1973.

UNIDO. Conference Proceedings on "Minimizing POllution from Fertilizer Plants." Helsinki, 1974.

WHO. *Health Hazards of the Human Environment.* Geneva, 1972.

WHO. *Safe Use of Pesticides.* Expert Committee on Insecticides Report #513. Geneva, 1973.

Wright, D.A., & Davison, A. W. "The Accumulation of Fluoride by Marine and Intertidal Animals." In *Environmental Pollution* 8(1–13), 1975.

Walters, H. *Nitrate in Soils & Plants & Animals.* Leicester, England: Blackfriars Press.

11

PLANT NUTRIENTS, BODY WASTE FERTILIZERS, AND AGRICULTURAL SANITATION

> Sanitation is a purely agricultural and biological question; it is not an engineering question and it is not a chemical question, and the more of engineering and chemistry we apply to sanitation, the more difficult the purifying agriculture. Our houses are flushed away but we pay for it by fouling every natural source of pure water.
>
> Dr. Vivian Poore*

It is an empirical fact that the problems involved in the disposal of body waste, especially from the health and agricultural standpoints, are world-wide.[1] During the first half of the nineteenth century, cholera and typhoid epidemics caused by water pollution constituted a serious threat to human life. Today, similarly, the scorge of environmental pollution not only threatens human life, but it also undermines the delicate

*Quoted in John Donkin, *Conservancy or Dry Sanitation versus Water Carriage* (London: Spon & Chamberlain, 1906).

balance of our global ecology. In its biological and chemical characteristics, the "crisis through water-borne pollution in London and some other large towns which led to the 'health movement' of the 1830's may be regarded as a forerunner of the crisis towards which the world is now moving."[2] With the exception of a few countries, the incidence of fecal-borne diseases such as dysentery, cholera, typhoid, and paratyphoid is so widespread that it constitutes a constant threat to public health in every continent. Public health authorities are already waging recurrent campaigns to limit the dangers of fecal pollution in rural and urban communities. However popular the campaigns may be, it appears certain that traditional anti-fecal-pollution public health measures, like applying a band aid to a festering sore, tend to achieve only marginal success. Unless a more effective means can be found soon to deal with these problems and be an integral part of a concerted attack on world hunger, population behavior in the foreseeable future will probably exacerbate the seriousness of an already discouraging global predicament. One of the most promising alternative solutions comes from the science of agricultural sanitation. Convincing experimental and field studies show agricultural sanitation to offer an inclusive means of dealing with the dual problems of health and agricultural productivity, in a systemic and perhaps most suitable manner.[3]

Winfield defines agricultural sanitation as ". . . the successful sanitation of the environment of man and his domestic animals by means which are an integral part of sound agricultural practice."[4] Properly interpreted, the applicability of agricultural sanitation is certainly not confined ". . . to farm sanitation, but covers a very much wider field and concerns city and town dwellers as intimately as those who live and work on the land."[5] Although the modern concept of agricultural sanitation was formulated at least some 50 years ago,[6] in practice it has remained grossly underrated and woefully underutilized in relation to its global potential. A basic method of implementing agricultural sanitation, to summarize from the technical and procedural details of the process, is through the conversion of body waste into pathogenically safe agro-nutrients. In this connection, it is relevant to reemphasize the global necessity of the conversion process and to provide the essential content for a global evaluation of its potentially valuable byproducts. Earlier chapters included the integration of relevant demographic, technocratic, biophysical, and biochemical data, and the formulation of an acceptable body waste/agronutrients conversion formula for certain specified national, regional, sub-global, and global material aggregates. For the world as a whole, a detailed separate treatment of each country's data and peculiarities would probably fill several volumes and is beyond the immediate scope of the present investigation. It is sufficient for the central purpose of this study that the geographic coverage of the survey is adequate to give useful information and practical ideas about the extent and magnitude of the problems involved in, as well as the potential benefits to be reaped from, the proper management of body waste.

The basic aggregates to be reviewed in this chapter and some of the relevant trends are presented in Tables 4.1, 5.1 and 5.2. The demographic figures from 1950 to 1975 cited in Table 4.1 indirectly determine the annual level and secular expansion of body waste material generated by human population alone, given man's normal absorptive capacity of his food intake. In 1950, for example, earth's 2.5 billion people produced an estimated 1.2 billion metric tons of fecal matter and related wastes. This averages out to a little less than 0.5 metric tons per person per year. More than 830 million metric tons of the total was accounted for by the developing world, and about 346 million metric tons by the developed world, or a subglobal ratio of about 2-1/2:1 respectively. The estimated nutrient content of the 1950 body waste was equivalent in magnitude to about 60 million metric tons of humuscite[7] with a minimum of 10.8 million metric tons of phosphorous, and 2.6 million metric tons of potassium. In monetary terms, the estimated value of the NPK nutrients, at 1975 world f.o.b. prices, is approximately $7 billion. In other words, in one year alone, the material equivalent of some 17.7 million metric tons of valuable NPK minerals was virtually wasted by traditional burying, burning, and aquatic dumping practices. It is not encouraging to observe that this mode of human behavior has remained unchanged during the last quarter-century, despite chronic shortages in postwar global consumption of agronutrients. For example, in 1960, 1970, and 1975, the corresponding amounts and values of unrecovered agronutrients are 21.2, 26.2, and 29.7 million metric tons valued at $8.4, $10.3, and $11.6 billion respectively (see Table 5.2). In the meantime, the economic and environmental costs of traditional body waste management practices are leading progressively to systemic crises of global proportions. Fortunately, environmental disasters can be minimizes, if not totally preventable. As a commitment to the conservational alternative to environmental disaster, it is necessary that the expected benefits of extracting vast quantities of agronutrients from global body waste should accrue to all segments of mankind. The developing and developed world communities together stand to realize permanently significant economic, social, and environmental benefits proportional to their numerical advantage should the science of agricultural sanitation be applied on a world-wide basis.

Based on Chinese experience and other empirical findings[8] the science of agricultural sanitation is effective in dealing with the dual problems of health and agricultural productivity, by providing the means of converting body waste safely into agronutrients. Members of an expanding global population can make a positive contribution to an equitable solution of the problem by mobilizing all resources at their command including and especially the vast quantity of agronutrients trapped in their own body waste. In the present global circumstances, such a bold anti-hunger resolution and practical commitment would be a welcome course of action. From this perspective, it appears that the global population problem is not entirely without a silver lining, despite its other dismal manifestations. For illustrative purposes, the potential magnitudes of recoverable agronutrients involved have been estimated and presented in Tables 8.1 and 8.2 for developed and developing world respectively, from 1950 to 1975, followed by a corresponding future projection from 1975 to 2000. These calculations indicate that the potential shares of developing countries in recoverable agronutrients (NPK) increased steadily over the last 25 years, from 12.4 (in 1950) to 21.2 million metric tons (in 1975). This represents a gross increase of about 9 million metric tons. The level of expansion during the first decade (1950 to 1960) and the last decade (1965 to 1975) contrasts sharply: the former was only about 2.8 million metric tons while the latter was at least 4.4 million metric tons. The quantitative difference between the two decades may be explained by a number of causal factors, among which better statistical reporting, higher life expectancy, low infant mortality, and increased food intake are among the most influential nutritional and demographic variables. In general, it is fair to conclude that the quantities of recoverable agronutrients potentially available to the developing world are not only substantial, but also compare favorably with indicated levels of chemical fertilizers used during the same postwar period. Experimental results have shown that the productivity of recoverable agronutrients compares impressively with that of synthetic chemical fertilizers.[9] In a recent investigation, experimental and field studies showed that where digested sludge was applied by ridge and furrow irrigation, crop yields were comparable or greater than those obtained with inorganic fertilizers applied at rates estimated to be adequate for maximum yields.[10] Among other findings and recommendations, the report concluded that "the use of a digested sludge as a source of nutrient for growing crops and as a soil amendment for reclaiming severely disturbed land is the most environmentally safe and economically sound to a growing solids waste handling problem. The cost and effort required for monitoring a digested sludge utilization, or land spreading operation to insure that adverse environmental impacts do not go undetected is rather small in comparison with the total benefits derived. . . . Control over potential pollutants is retained where emphasis is on sludge utilization rather than its disposal."[11] It may be inferred from available empirical findings that the aggregate level of agricultural and food production in the developing world would most probably have increased substantially if their use of agronutrients had been augmented by as much organic fertilizers as the human population in those areas could provide by converting their body waste into agronutrients. To better underline the economic value of some of the magnitudes involved, it may be noted in Table 8.2 that, as imports valued at 1975 world f.o.b. prices, the corresponding amounts of recoverable NPK agronutrients would have cost the developing world as much as $4.9 billion in 1950, $5.4 billion in 1955, $6.0 billion in 1960, $6.6 billion in 1965, $7.6 billion in 1970, and $8.3 billion in 1975. Needless to say, to many countries in the developing world plagued by chronic balance-of-payments deficits and threatened by international financial bankruptcy, the real value of being able to produce badly needed agronutrients from domestic body waste (resources) is far greater than that reflected by international market prices alone.

From the perspective of the developed world, the economic, social, and environmental benefits of applied agricultural sanitation, especially of converting body waste into agronutrients, are without doubt significant. Our calculations in Table 8.1 show that the amounts of NPK nutrients potentially recoverable from indicated levels of body waste are 4.8 million metric tons in 1950, 5.8 million metric tons in 1960, 7.1 million metric tons in 1970, and 8.5 million metric tons in 1975. Between 1950 and 1975, the gross change in the annual figures was 3.6 million metric tons, which is quite small when averaged over the relevant period of 25 years. The corresponding level of expansion during the first decade (1950 to 1960) was only 0.95 million metric tons. In the last decade (1965 to 1975) the gross change was 2.01 million metric tons. From these indications, it may be concluded that for the developed world communities, the annual amounts of potentially recoverable agronutrients are quite modest by global standards. Finally, by comparing decadal changes in potential levels of recoverable agronutrients, the indicated quantities for the developed world represent only 34 percent and 45 percent of the corresponding amounts for the developing world during the 1950 to 1960 and 1965 to 1975 subperiods. The lower rates of potential output in the developed world may be due in part to the relative inactivity of growth-inducing demographic factors, particularly on the European continent as a whole, in the immediate postwar decades. Nevertheless, the economic values of the quinquennial figures (for the developed world) are substantial. In monetary terms, the corresponding amounts of NPK nutrients valued at 1975 world f.o.b. prices would cost about $1.9 billion in 1950, $2.0 billion in 1955, $2.3 billion in 1960, $2.5 billion in 1965, $2.8 billion in 1970, and $3.2 billion in 1975. Obviously, the cumulative burden of such growing financial transactions payable in "hard" or "soft" international currency becomes progressively heavier over time. In the present circumstances, however, it is important to realize that the imputed values do not represent debits but potential savings in domestic resources or in foreign exchange available to the developed world communities.

For the world as a whole, the magnitude of potential losses directly sustained over the past 25 years by the failure to recover displaced NPK resources trapped in body waste alone is conservatively estimated at more than $250 billion or an average of about $10 billion per year. In physical terms, the real loss corresponds to the potential for increased food and agricultural production lost by the systemic failure to reclaim and utilize body waste agronutrients. In the last analysis, both the surviving victims and those immune from the global tragedy of world hunger must realize that greater amounts of such displaced resources will continue to be lost in the future,[12] should present waste management practices continue unchanged in the world. In this sense, the indicated magnitudes of potentially unrecovered NPK resources constitute a simple measure—but an ugly index—of unnecessary wastefulness for which mankind is shamefully and regrettably responsible.

NOTES

1. J. S. Simmons et al., *Global Epidemiology*, A Geography of Disease and Sanitation (London: Heineman, 1944); Sepp Endel, *The Use of Sewage for Irrigation* (California State Department of Public Health, 1963); Sim Van der Ryn, *The Toilet Papers*; J. C. Scott, *Health and Agriculture in China*; WHO, *Composting: Sanitary Disposal and Reclamation of Organic Wastes*, 1956; WHO, "Community Water Supply and Wastewater Disposal," in *WHO Chronical* vol. 30 no. 8 (1976).

2. Conference on Law, Science and Politics, *Water Pollution As a World Problem* (London: Europa Publications, 1970), p. 153.

3. FAO, *Organic Materials as Fertilizers*; *Organic Materials and Soil Productivity*; *China: Recycling of Organic Wastes*; J. C. Scott, op. cit.; G. F. Winfield, "Studies on the Control of Fecal-borne Diseases in North China," in *Chinese Medical Journal* 48 (1934); Sim Van der Ryn, *The Toilet Papers*, op. cit.

4. J. C. Scott, op. cit., p. 21.

5. Ibid.

6. A. Howard, "The Waste Products of Agriculture and their Utilization as Humus," in *Royal Sco. Art. Report* (December, 1933); F. K. Jackson, and Y. D. Wad, "The Sanitary Disposal and Agricultural Utilization of Habitation Wastes by the Indore Process," *Indore Bulletin* #1, (Inst. Plant Breed., 1934); J. C. Scott, op. cit.

7. See Chapter 6 and Table 5.1.

8. N. R. Stoll, "On the Economic Value of Night Soil in China," *American Journal of Hygiene*, monog. 7 (1926); F. H. King, *Farmers for Forty Centuries*; FAO *China, Recycling . . .* op. cit.; A. C. Garg, et al., *Organic Manures*; FAO *Organic Manures As Fertilizers*; T. D. Hinesly, *Agricultural Benefits and Environmental Changes. . .*, loc. cit; OECD, *Effective Use of Fertilizers*, loc. cit.; FAO, *Organic Recycling in Asia and the Pacific*, loc. cit.; P. L. Jaiswal, *Handbook of Manures and Fertilizers*, New Delhi; I.C.A.R. 1977; FAO, *Organic Manures and Soil Productivity*, op. cit.

9. T. D. Hinesly, op. cit.; FAO, *China Recycling . . .*; A. C. Garg, et al., op. cit.; G. C. W. Ames, "Can Organic Manures Improve Crop Production in Southern India?", *Compost Science*, 17 no 2 (1976); FAO, *Organic Materials and Soil Productivity*, op. cit.

10. T. D. Hinesly, op. cit., p. 1.

11. Ibid., p. 5.

12. See Tables 5.1, 5.2, 8.1 and 8.2 for numerical projections.

FURTHER READING

Allison, F. E. *Soil Organic Matter and Its Role in Crop Production*. New York: Elsevier Scientific Publ. Co., 1973.

Balfour, E. B. *The Living Soil*. London: Faber & Faber, 1942.

Bennett, H. H. *Soil Conservation.* New York: McGraw-Hill, 1939.

FAO. *Organic Materials as Fertilizers.* Soils Bull. 27. Rome, 1975.

———. *Organic Materials and Soil Productivity.* Soils. Bull. 35. Rome, 1977.

Economics of Sludge Applications Systems on Agricultural Lands. Davis, Ca.: AgWest Inc., 1974.

Goldstein, J. *Sensible Sludge.* A New Look at A Wasted Resource. Emmaus, PA.: Rodale Press, 1977.

Golueke, C. *Composting.* Emmaus, PA.: Rodale Press, 1972.

Gloyna, E. *Waste Stabilization Ponds.* WHO. Geneva, 1971.

Peterson, J. R., et al., "Human and Animal Wastes As Fertilizers." In *Fertilizer Technology and Use,* 2nd ed. Madison, Wisc.: SSSA, 1971.

Purris, J. E., et al., *The Chemical Examination of Water, Sewage, Food, and Other Substances.* Cambridge: Cambridge University Press, 1914.

Van Vuren, J. P. J. *Soil Fertility and Sewage.* New York: Dover, 1949.

Wheeler, H. J. *Manures and Fertilizers.* New York: Mcmillan & Co., 1914.

WHO. *Composting: Sanitary Disposal and Reclamation of Organic Wastes.* Geneva, 1958.

12

THE WASTE OF NATIONS AND GLOBAL AGRICULTURAL UNDERDEVELOPMENT

Humanity feels fastidious and shrinks away from any prolonged contamination with filth of organic origin. We know in our bones that it is waste. What we have now to establish as the thought and practice of responsible people is that the time has come when the complete utilization of organic wastes must so be ensured as to supply humanity with its food and with most of its raw materials.

L. J. Picton*

The human population cannot survive without a continuous supply of energy to perform the vital functions necessary to the maintenance of life. Man's intake of food, water, and air are transformed into appropriate chemical nutrients, the vital fuel supplies destined for biochemical consumption in the body. As part of the natural functions of the metabolic process, the unassimilated residuals of the intake are eliminated from the

*Nutrition and the Soil (New York: Devin-Adair Co., 1949), p. 34.

body.[1] The social impact of the mass of the human body waste so produced is basically determined by the degree of success achieved in eliminating the volatility (hyperactivity) of its chemical and bacterial constituents. The chemical nature and ecological effects of human body waste in socio-ecosystems have been discussed in Chapters 5 and 6. The most crucial factor determining the effective rate of elimination of body waste in the socio-ecosystem is the degree of harmonious interaction between the prevailing man-made rules and the natural ecological rules of the game. For example, without proper handling, the noxious and pathological effects of decomposition may constitute serious threats to public health and well-being, especially in densely populated socio-eco-systems. In today's world of proliferating cities and urban megalopoli, body waste-related problems are merely sub-merged but not eliminated. As the geopolitical frame of reference expands into complex continental and global di-mensions, the basic problems demand, more than ever, serious attention and forward-looking solutions, not cosmetic treat-ments.

What, then, is the central issue—too many people, too little food, or too much waste? Obviously, the central issue is composed of more than the three preceding elements. It is a many-sided global crisis in which excessive inequality, ex-cessive procreation, and excessive waste are among the in-auspicious factors at work. If one is to avoid many of the past mistakes in dealing with such issues, the present situation must be treated as a process rather than a terminal point in one-dimensional problem space. Looking at the crisis through the window of the world food shortage has been a necessary and rewarding simplification of a complex issue. At close range, the problems and possibilities of augmenting the supply of man's food seem to enlarge in progressive stages. In the magnified state, one of the major inputs—agronutrients—has been isolated for special and extensive review as it appears to offer the widest latitude of substitutability in global food and agricultural production functions.

In most agricultural systems, the basic motivation behind high intensive fertilization is to increase or maintain high productivity per crop-acre, other things remaining equal. As indicated earlier, available global evidence shows that extreme variations prevail in productivity per acre for similar crops. This is due particularly, though not exclusively, to the wide variation in fertilizer consumption in different geographic areas and agricultural systems. The lack of adequate agronutrients in agricultural productivity is seldom unambiguous and rarely disastrous in the short run. Furthermore, the early symptoms may be confused with other manifestations of soil ailments. The phenomenon of global deficiency in consumption of agronutrients results in part from, and is symptomatic of, the usual spasms of uncontrollable market failures as well as the inefficacy of supplemental nonmarket mechanisms for dealing with severe shortages in local places. In advanced or chronic stages of agronutrient deficiencies, the agricultural enterprises being affected usually reveal physical signs of degeneration. From that vulnerable state, further deterioration merely hastens the descent first into marginal agriculture, next into bankruptcy, and eventually to the abandonment of farming. Although such degenerative tendencies also occur in developed countries, the process is far more common in the less-developed countries.

In the larger context of world economic and social development, it appears that the problem of global agricultural underdevelopment is structurally linked to the phenomenon of disguised deficiencies in the global consumption of agronutrients. Some aspects of the linkage may be obvious. To begin with, substantial deficiencies of agronutrients occurring over a prolonged period would normally be accompanied by significant amounts of factor employment distortions. This, in turn, would imply an imbalance of varying degrees in factor combinations in different areas of agricultural production. If the resulting imbalance in factor-mix were to remain uncorrected, it would induce appropriate factor employment gaps in relevant agricultural activity. Beyond factor employment distortions, any additive effects of production displacements would tend to result in suboptimal rate of output growth. In such advanced situations, the asymptote of a curve formed by the collection of suboptimal growth points would sufficiently describe a path of underdevelopment equilibrium.

The exact magnitudes of actual deficiencies in global agronutrient consumption are difficult to determine. Tentative estimates based on world fertilizer consumption figures, however, suggest varying amounts ranging approximately from six to eight million metric tons annually, during the first half of the seventies. On the average, this quantity is equivalent in magnitude to about ten percent of the corresponding global fertilizer consumption figures, and is quite substantial by any relevant standards. It is particularly important to realize that roughly eight-tenths of the indicated global deficiency originates in the less-developed countries. Moreover, in relation to their respective global shares, consumption shortages attributable to the less-developed countries are equivalent in magnitude to about 50 percent of their aggregate consumption figures, whereas the corresponding figures for the developed countries is only 4.9 percent. Reliable numerical estimates for the early postwar period, especially the fifties, are extremely difficult, if not impossible to make because of the paucity of detailed statistical information. In view of the experience of the first half of the seventies, however, reasonable interpolation of corresponding figures for the fifties and sixties seem to suggest that disguised shortages in consumption were integral parts of the postwar global trend.

As a fraction of the world's total agricultural land, the comparative size of the areas being affected by deficient consumption of agronutrients is extremely large, and, in human terms, it is the geographic home of more than two-thirds of the world's population. Because of the overwhelming proportion of agricultural areas and people affected, the cumulative effects of deficient fertilizer consumption over the last two decades have inevitably dragged world agriculture and food production into depressed states of underdevelopmental equilibria, despite substantial postwar expansion in agricultural output. As long as that condition prevails, balanced global agricultural development will be hampered by the cumulative impact of the negative constraints.

It is appropriate to call attention to some of the negative welfare implications of global agricultural underdevelopment on the distribution side. It is clear from the present state of the world that the social impact of extreme inequality casts an ominous shadow over the world community. By civilized standards of decency, it is intolerable that millions of the peoples in less-developed countries who suffer famine, starvation, and hunger deaths are forced to make supreme sacrifices, while others continue to exploit and expropriate world agricultural and food resources beyond reasonable limits and equitable propriety. Former West German Chancellor Willy Brandt put this predicament succinctly in an address delivered to audiences from Cambridge and Boston in March 1977, when he declared: "Justice demands—and even if we do not want to listen to justice, reason will tell us—that there will never be a lasting and secure co-existence of affluence and misery." With due regard to the human costs associated with conditions of agricultural underdevelopment, an inescapable question arises: is the world community able and willing to reduce effectively and eventually eliminate existing deficiencies in global consumption of agronutrients? There are numerous answers to this question, but only one inclusive solution to the basic problem. As indicated earlier, the candidate solution entails the creation of appropriate technologies to facilitate the monetization of nutrients trapped in body waste. This process inevitably involves the transformation of wastes into economic goods of comparatively high social utility—the agronutrients. If this were to be accomplished, the effective transformation of body waste from a simple ecological resource to an economic resource would be successfully completed, and pave the way to a safe absorption of the products by the socio-ecosystem.

The body waste problem is a unique example of resource

displacement in socio-ecosystems. To resolve the problem effectively, man would do well to learn from and work with nature. Unlike other organic sources of minerals for agro-nutrients, the chemical constituents of body waste represent a permanent source of renewable materials guaranteed by the human metabolic system. It is regrettable that since the creation of Adam and Eve, people have viewed the flow of body waste through highly distorted channels of observation: superstition, fear, uncertainty, and now, exasperation. It is particularly relevant, in this context, to recall the observation of J. B. Lawes that ". . . the Almighty has endowed the same particles of matter with the property of entering into a variety of forms; at one time the most offensive, and at another time the most attractive. In this ever changing circle, nothing is without its value, nothing is lost." Despite its complexity and changing appearance, matter is—in its infinitely interconnected phases or forms of biotic and abiotic existence—one and the same. Thus, the monetization of body waste nutrients is not only in line with the circular flow of material transformations, it is a necessary extension of conventional economic and accounting principles which deal with the circular flow of economic activity.

Most well-defined practical and theoretical problems usually have optimal solutions. When one views the body waste problem from the total perspective, an optimal solution is not likely to be found merely by imposing backward-looking solutions, however convenient and economical they may seem at present. The search for an optimal solution must begin with the recovery of our intrinsic force of scientific detachment and the mental preparedness to look at the whole problem anew and in greater detail. Given the nature of the body waste problem, an optimal solution will neither be found nor recognized until man accepts the means available for dealing with it without atavistic self-consciousness. There is no shame in recovering material values trapped temporarily in the global flow of human metabolic waste. As in most complex social problems, man's misperceptions and negative attitudes toward human body waste may yet prove to be the most difficult obstacles to the dawning of enlightened global awareness and action. The average person regards body waste as a necessary evil, an embarrassment to be tolerated and treated as anti-life matter, even though the elimination of such wastes is a natural life-sustaining process.

Figures 3.1 and 3.2 illustrated alternative schemes of materials flow in a socio-ecosystem, and of the natural processes of material transformation envisaged. Both models feature simplified systems in which the processing of body waste and the recovery of agronutrients are integrated. In Figure 3.1, waste processing is based on *aerobic procedures*; in Figure 3.2, it is based on *anaerobic procedures*. As indicated in Chapter 7, the basic differences between aerobic and anaerobic processes are the means by which the microbial population is maintained with and without the supply of oxygen. The essential features of *aerobic processes* "are that a population of microorganisms is maintained, the waste is brought in contact with the mass of microorganisms, and oxygen is supplied at a rate high enough that they may carry out their metabolic activities in an aerobic environment."[2] The output of the process consists of inorganic oxidation products such as ammonia, sulfates, phosphates, and humus. *Anaerobic digestion* "is a process by which a portion of the organic matter of a concentrated waste is oxidized biologically in the absence of molecular oxygen."[3] The microorganisms that carry out the decomposition utilize certain oxidizing agents that include nitrates, sulfates, carbonates, and some of the organic compounds originally present. The output of anaerobic digestion includes carbon dioxide, water, ammonia, molecular nitrogen, methane, and other reduced organic compounds. Figures 3.1 and 3.2 are particular examples of the numerous ways in which matter can be transformed from one state to another in continuous cyclical flow of material processes. Figure 12.1 illustrates the linkages of man, body waste, agronutrients, and crops. Despite its obvious simplification, the idea is illuminating in the limited context of the subject being discussed. Finally, the essential elements of Figures 3.1, 3.2 and 12.1 have been combined in a flow diagram—Figure 12.2—to recapitulate the key elements of the proposed scheme for solving the body waste problem. The relationships expressed in the flow diagram are summarized in four short statements: 1) human population provides body waste (excretes metabolic residue from food intake; 2) body waste provides the raw materials for conversion into agro-nutrients; 3) agronutrients provide fertilizers for plants and soils (to facilitate large-scale crop production; and 4) crops provide the raw materials for man's food.

The variety of methods and techniques being applied in different countries are differentiated between the aerobic and anaerobic systems. For example, the Chinese method of composting body waste includes wide-ranging variations of the aerobic process in which body waste, animal feces, garbage, and soil are combined, sometimes equally by weight, sometimes in variable proportions.[4] The whole pile (material-mix) is completely covered with earth and allowed to undergo

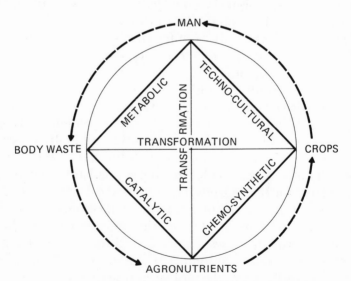

Figure 12.1 A Circular Flow of Material Transformation

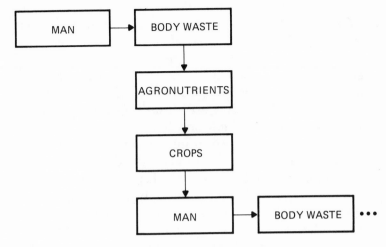

Figure 12.2 A Flow Diagram of Material Processes

aerobic decomposition for about five weeks, during which the enteric parasites and most of the pathogenic bacteria are destroyed. The compost is then collected and applied to the fields. In India, the "Indore and Bangalore" process of composting developed and popularized in the 1930s by Sir Albert Howard has continued to be applied extensively with little or no modifications. This process has been adapted for body waste composting.[5] The essential raw materials—night soil and leaves—are combined in specified proportions, covered with earth, and allowed to decompose in an aerobic environment for a period of about eight months. The residual compost is collected and restored to the soil. In recent years, anaerobic methods of processing body waste have been used increasingly, along with the well-established Indore process.

In contrast to the preceding examples, some countries, notably Vietnam, Tanzania, and Mozambique, are developing new devices for on-the-spot composting. In the sixties, the government of Vietnam designed and installed the double-vault excreta-composting septic tank,[6] as a part of its rural hygiene campaign. When the tank is about two-thirds full, the hole is filled to the brim with dried powdered earth and the container is tightly closed to create an anaerobic environment. After decomposing for 45 days, all bacteria and pathogenic viruses are reportedly destroyed. The residual substance is rich in fertilizer and is restored to the soil. In Mozambique, a double-vault system (the BIOPOT) for composting excreta has recently been developed in the continuing search for effective solutions to water pollution and body waste disposal problems.[7] This device is different from the Vietnamese in that the BIOPOT employs aerobic methods. The Tanzanian government is currently testing a new waste disposal system, compost latrines, as a part of the national hygiene campaign. A preliminary report evaluating the effectiveness and acceptability of the device is encouraging.[8] Sweden and other Scandinavian countries have had some success with sewerless compost toilets, and these are receiving increasing attention in other European countries. In Canada and the United States, some of the existing Swedish designs (the Clivus Multrum, for example) and a variety of other new devices are being developed and tested for both rural and urban areas. Encouraging as these developments may be, they hardly constitute a trend for the world community as a whole.

Nevertheless, it is of particular interest to note that the experience of China and India in restoring processed human waste to the soil is more genuinely national in scope and far more advanced than any comparable programs currently underway in any other part of the world. Compared to the well-established programs of China and India, Canada and the United States are barely beyond the experimental stages. For the world as a whole, fewer than one-fifth of the countries are conducting some form of research and development even at the modest levels existing in Canada and the United States. These are a few of the attempts being made to solve the problems connected with fecal-borne diseases and waste disposal in various countries. The overwhelming majority of countries have yet to embark on systematic research into this field. We share the hope expressed decades ago by one of the modern pioneers in this field:

> The time is probably now ripe for a much larger and more co-ordinated attack on these problems, and the knowledge which is by now available ought to make it possible to describe more fully and clearly the purview of Agricultural Sanitation. It should also make clear the contribution that Agricultural Sanitation can make towards meeting the steadily developing problems of World Hunger. The principles are clear, the techniques can be mastered, and willing men and women of determination and goodwill could use them for the benefit of mankind. Where are these men and women?[10]

RECOMMENDATION: A GLOBAL AUTHORITY ON WASTE ELIMINATION AND RECONVERSION

Certainly a more substantial effort can and should be devoted to solving, once and for all, the threatening problems associated with the global flow of primary waste. The world community must forge a unified global response to the increasingly serious threats emanating from body waste pollution of surface and subsurface waters, soils, and the spacial environment on which human life and survival ultimately depends. To secure maximum natural advantages of a unified global solution to problems created by the waste of nations, the following program of action is deemed necessary and is strongly recommended:

1. The establishment of a Global Authority on Waste Elimination and Reconversion, under the United Nations, to coordinate necessary national programs and promote, induce, and accelerate the development of socially and technologically optimal recoversion systems for designated categories of

displaced resources; in particular, the primary waste of nations. The goals of the Authority should include the following: a) worldwide mobilization of abundant non-conventional, energy efficient resources trapped in body waste; b) the elimination of global agricultural underdevelopment due to chronic deficiency and underconsumption of fertilizers by the majority of world farmers; c) an optimal management of the progressively critical imbalance between world population behavior and limited food supply capabilities; and d) the elimination of environmental pollution originating from conventional practices of primary waste disposal.

2. The compilation of data on body waste reconversion devices now available or being tested anywhere in the world, including specific conditions for which devices are designed (such as climate, soil, hydrology, etc.); production costs of devices; energy and water required to operate; and results of controlled agricultural applications of residual agronutrients.

3. In the event that this global data (carefully assembled and monitored) should demonstrate clearly that no devices currently available are adequate to hasten the achievement of the aforementioned objective goals, it is further recommended that the United Nations should, forthwith, direct the Authority to assemble a Special Emergency Global Task Force of Experts on Waste Elimination and Reconversion. The prime assignment of the task force is to search for and provide applicable and practical solutions to body waste reconversion and management problems for rural and urban areas, using the data already assembled to identify candidate leads for intensive research on, and development of, appropriate technologies and devices. Since no single device would serve such structurally disparate social spaces equally well, the presumption is strong that the task force will find a variety of solutions to the problem. (In view of the critical importance of the time element, it is reasonable to expect completion of the said assignment well within five years).

In the larger context of human relations, body waste is not just another renewable source of materials for agronutrients. It is important not to lose sight of its symbolic mystique—every human being participates as an equal in its creation. No groups of people or countries are "more developed" or "less developed," "rich" or "poor" in producing body waste. The bottom line is that, unlike many antiegalitarian facts of life, this common biological work is one of the few free functions that nature itself calls upon man to perform. Better that man should profit from nature's command!

From the economic point of view, it makes good sense that all agronutrients extractable from body waste should supplement other types of fertilizers which aid in expanding world food and agricultural production. Above all, from the point of view of environmental sanitation, such action would be a step toward the eventual reduction or replacement of synthetic fertilizer. However small in relation to total world requirements, the additional quantity of agronutrients obtainable from the national flow of body waste should make some difference between the actual and potential numbers of people who otherwise might suffer starvation and death. Viewed in the global context of the North-South dialogue, the potential beneficiaries of the proposed action include not just those communities suffering the worst effects of fertilizer and food shortages, but—by helping to increase the global capability to grow more food and agricultural produce, and lending support to global peace and stability—the entire human population!

The world community has a vested interest in promoting domestic, international, and global measures that would ensure the practicality and success of necessary programs. It would be a tragic mistake, with serious if not dire consequences for mankind, should special interests and institutional adversaries oppose and delay implementation of such measures to the extent that their adoption would come too late to be of real help in rectifying some of the inherent ills of this potentially dangerous and cataclysmic world. On the critical issue of how to provide more fertilizers and more food for the world population, the time is long overdue for mankind to make a moral commitment: to declare a holy war on starvation and poverty. However late, there is time enough for mankind to resolve that "Never Again" shall man tolerate the intolerable— man's inhumanity to man—symbolized by welfare trade-offs which do little in contemporary international economic and political relations to eradicate famine, starvation, and deaths for the many while increasing material affluence for the few. No more potentially worthwhile solution awaits the world community in its attempts to prepare for the unknown challenges of the twenty-first century.

NOTES

1. The first part of the metabolic output is used up for general maintenance, growth, and development of life from the simplest manifestations to the complex dimensions. Once eliminated from the body, the second part (of the metabolic output) adds materially to the permanent flow of human body waste present in the socio-ecosystem.

2. W. O. Pipes, *Waste-Recovery Processes for a Closed Ecological System*, Panel on Closed Ecological Systems, Armed Forces-NRC Committee on BioAstronautics (Washington, D.C.: National Academy of Sciences, 1961), p. 14.

3. Ibid., p. 12.

4. FAO, *China: Recycling of Organic Wastes in Agriculture*, Soils Bulletin 40 (Rome, Chinese Medical Journal, 1975; Peoples Hygiene Publisher, *Compilation of Data on Experience and Sanitary Management of Excreta and Urine in the Village*, trans. L. T. Loy, unpublished report of the International Development Research Centre, Ottawa, Canada; Roger Blobaum, "China Recycles Her Wastes by Using Them on the Land," in *Compost Science*, vol. 16 no. 5 (1975); F. H. King, *Farmers of Forty Centuries* (New York: Harcourt, Brace, 1927); J. C. Scott, *Health and Agriculture in China* (London: Faber & Faber, Ltd., 1953).

5. Sir Albert Howard, *An Agricultural Testament* (London: Oxford University Press, 1940); A. C. Garg et al., *Organic Manures* (New Delhi: ICAR, 1971); H. B. Gottas, *Composting*, WHO Monograph 31 (Geneva, 1956); M. V. Bopardikar, "Optimum Utilization of Compost in India;" A. Makhijani and A. Poole, *Energy and Agriculture in the Third World* (Cambridge, Mass.: Ballinger Co., 1976), chapter 4; P. L. Jaiswal, *Handbook of Manures and Fertilizers* (New Delhi: ICAR, 1971); FAO *Organic Materials and Soil Productivity*, Soils Bulletin 35 (Rome, 1977).

6. J. K. McMichael, *Health in the Third World—Studies from Vietnam* (Nottingham, England: Spokesman Books, 1976).

7. For details see OXFAM Conference on Sanitation for the Developing Nations, Oxford, England: Proceedings of Conference (summer 1977);

Harold Leich, "Sanitation for the Developing Nations," in *Compost Science* 18 no 5 (1977); also see 19 no 5 (1978).

8. Ronald Gurak et al., "Compost Latrines in Tanzania: A Preliminary Report," *Compost Science* 18 no. 4 (1977).

9. J. C. Scott, *Health and Agriculture in China*, p. 255.

FURTHER READING

Cole, H. S. et al., eds. *Thinking About the Future*. New York: Chatto and Windus for Sussex Univ. Press, 1973.

Garvey, G. *Energy, Ecology, Economy*. New York: Norton, 1972.

Gorden, M., and Gorden, M., eds. *Environmental Management*. Boston: Allyn & Bacon, 1972.

Gregory, R. *The Price of Amenity*. London: Macmillan, 1971.

Harte, J. A., & Socolow, R. H., eds. *The Patient Earth*. New York: Holt, Rinehart & Winston, 1971.

Hinricks, N., ed. *Population, Environment, and People*. New York: McGraw-Hill, 1971.

Kay, D. A., & Skolnikoff, E. B. *World Eco-crisis: International Organizations in Response*. Madison: Univ. of Wisconsin Press, 1972.

Linneman, H., et al. *MOIRA: Model of International Relations in Agriculture*. Amsterdam: North Holland Pub. Co., 1976.

O'Riordan, T. *Perspectives on Resource Management*. London: Pion Press, 1971.

Odum, H. T. *Environment, Power and Society*. New York: John Wiley & Sons, 1971.

Page, T. *Economics of Involuntary Transfers: A Unified Approach to Pollution and Congestion Externalities*. New York: Springer-Verlag, 1973.

Schurr, S. H., ed. *Energy Economic Growth and the Environment*. Baltimore: Johns Hopkins Press, 1972.

Study of Critical Environmental Problems. *Man's Impact on the Global Environment: Assessment and Recommendation for Action*. MIT, 1970.

Lord Walston. *Dealing with Hunger*. London: The Bodley Head, 1976.

Ward, B., & Dubos, Rene. *Only One Earth*. Hammondworth: Penguin Books, 1972.

APPENDICES

APPENDIX A

TABLES: PRINCIPAL SOURCES

Table 4.1: Estimated from global population and human metabolic output data. See *UN Demographic Yearbook 1975*; J. B. Lawes, *The Sewage of London*; P. J. Cammidge, *The Feces of Children and Adults*, pp. 6–7; R. C. Rendtorf, "Stool Patterns of Healthy Adult Males"; D. P. Burkitt, 1971 and 1972; M. A. Eastwood, "Effects of Dietary Supplements. . ."; Sunderman & Boerner, "Feces," in *Normal Values*; A. C. Garg, *Organic Manures*; J. McHale, *World Facts and Trends*.

Table 5.1: Estimates are based on data and definitions in J. B. Lawes (1855), pp. 18–27; FAO, *Organic Materials as Fertilizers*, pp. 20–24; A. C. Garg, *Organic Manures*, pp. 9–10, 27–28; D. P. Burkitt, 1971 and 1972; Rendtorf and Kashagarian (1967); P. J. Cammidge, 1914; and Sunderman and Boerner, "Feces" in *Normal Values*.

Table 5.2: Principal sources of estimation are USDA, *Fertilizer Situation-1977*; FAO, *Monthly Bulletin of Agricultural Economics and Statistics*; USDA, *World Fertilizer Review and Prospects to 1980/81*; UN-FAO, "Longer-Term Fertilizer Supply/Demand Position and Elements of a World Fertilizer Policy," AGS:F/75/7 (May 1975); FAO Commission on Fertilizers, 2nd Session, Rome, June 3–7, 1975; British Sulphur Corporation, *Fertilizer International*, 89 (November 1976), p. 5; UN-FAO, "Current Situation and Longer Term Outlook," FAO Commission on Fertilizers, Third Session (Rome, June 8–11), prepared by the FAO/UNIDA/World Bank Group on Fertilizers; UN-FAO, *Organic Material as*

Fertilizers, chapter 3; J. J. C. Van Voorhoeve, "Organic Fertilizers; Problems and Potentials for Developing Countries." in IBRD Fertilizer Study (Washington, D.C., 1974).

Tables 5.3 FAO, *Annual Fertilizer Review* (Rome, 1950–1976); FAO, & 5.4 *Monthly Bulletin of Agricultural Economics & Statistics* (January–December, 1976); USDA, *World Fertilizer Review and Prospects to 1980/81*; USDA, *1977 Fertilizer Situation* (Washington, D.C.: Economic Research, January 1977).

Table 8.1: Same as Tables 5.1 and 5.2.

Table 8.2: Ibid.

Table 8.3: FAO, *Organic Materials as Fertilizers*, pp. 19–71; A. C. Garg, *Organic Manures*, pp. 2–14; D. P. Hopkins, *Chemicals, Humus, and the Soil*, pp. 111–132; J. J. C. Van Voorhoeve, "Organic Fertilizers: Problems and Potentials for Developing Countries"; L. P. Jaisal, *Handbook of Manures and Fertilizers*.

Table 8.4: Ibid.

Table 8.5: Ibid.

Table 8.6: Ibid.

Table 8.7: Ibid.

APPENDIX B

REGIONAL COMPOSITION OF GEOGRAPHIC AREAS

AFRICA

North Africa
West Africa
East Africa
Middle Africa
South Africa

ASIA

Southwest Asia
Middle South Asia
Southeast Asia
East Asia

EUROPE

Northern Europe
Western Europe
Eastern Europe
Southern Europe
Union of Soviet Socialist Republics

AMERICA

North America
Middle South America
Tropical South America
Temperate South America
Caribbean

OCEANIA

NATIONAL COMPOSITION: AFRICA

NORTH AFRICA

Algeria
Egypt
Libya
Morocco
Sudan
Tunisia

WEST AFRICA

Cape Verde Islands
Benin (formerly Dahomey)
Gambia
Ghana
Guinea
Ivory Coast
Liberia
Mali
Mauritania
Niger
Nigeria
Guinea-Bissau
   (formerly Port Guinea)
Senegal
Sierra-Leone
Togo
Upper Volta

EAST AFRICA

Burundi
Comoro Islands
Ethiopia
Kenya
Malagasy Republic
Malawi
Mauritius
Mozambique
Reunion
Rhodesia
Rwanda
Somalia
Tanzania
Uganda
Zambia

MIDDLE AFRICA

Angola
Cameroon
Central African Empire
Chad
Congo
Equatorial Guinea
Gabon
Zaire

SOUTH AFRICA

Botswana
Lesotho
Republic of South Africa
Namibia
Swaziland

NATIONAL COMPOSITION: ASIA

SOUTHWEST ASIA

Bahrain
Cyprus
Gaza
Iraq
Israel
Jordan
Kuwait
Lebanon
Oman
Qatar
Saudi Arabia
Syria
Turkey
U. A. Emirates
Yemen Arab Republic
Yemen Dem. Republic

MIDDLE SOUTH ASIA

Afghanistan
Bangladesh
Bhutan
India
Iran
Maldive Islands
Nepal
Pakistan
Sikkim
Sri Lanka

SOUTHEAST ASIA

Burma
Indonesia
Khmer Republic
Laos
Malaysia
Philippines
Singapore
Thailand
Socialist Republic of Vietnam

EAST ASIA

China
Hong Kong
Japan
Korea, Dem. Rep. of
Korea, Republic of
Macau
Mongolia
Taiwan

NATIONAL COMPOSITION: EUROPE

NORTHERN EUROPE

Denmark
Finland
Iceland
Ireland
Norway
Sweden
United Kingdom

WESTERN EUROPE

Austria
Belgium
France
Fed. Rep. of Germany
Luxembourg
Netherlands
Switzerland

EASTERN EUROPE

Bulgaria
Czechoslovakia
Dem. Rep. of Germany
Hungary
Poland
Romania

SOUTHERN EUROPE

Albania
Greece
Italy
Malta
Portugal
Spain
Yugoslavia

UNION OF SOVIET SOCIALIST REPUBLICS

NATIONAL COMPOSITION: AMERICA

NORTH AMERICA

Canada
United States of America

MIDDLE
SOUTH AMERICA

Costa Rica
El Salvador
Guatemala
Honduras
Mexico
Nicaragua
Panama

TEMPERATE
SOUTH AMERICA

Argentina
Chile
Paraguay
Uruguay

TROPICAL
SOUTH AMERICA

Bolivia
Brazil
Colombia
Ecuador
Guyana
Peru
Surinam
Venezuela

CARIBBEAN

Bahamas
Barbados
Cuba
Dominican Republic
Guadeloupe
Haiti
Jamaica
Martinique
Netherlands Antilles
Puerto Rico
Trinidad/Tobago

NATIONAL COMPOSITION: OCEANIA

OCEANIA

Australia
Fiji
New Zealand
Papua/New Guinea
Smaller Islands & Enclaves

Sources: National Geographic Society, *Atlas of the World*, 4th ed. (Washington, D.C., 1975); Hamond, Inc., *World Atlas* (New Jersey, 1971); The Environmental Fund, *World Population Estimates—1975* (Washington, D.C., 1975).

INDEX

About the Author

Dr. Fahm, who holds a PhD in industrial economics from the Massachusetts Institute of Technology, has served as Senior Economist and Assistant Director of Research at the United Nations Institute for Training and Research, New York. He was professor of economics and acting dean of the Faculty of Social Science at the University of Lagos and has taught in a number of American universities, including the State University of New York, the Massachusetts Institute of Technology, and the universities of California and Connecticut. At present he is the Senior Economist at ECORESA International. He has also been a consultant to international organizations, state economic development agencies and private manufacturing firms, and has been widely published in books and professional journals.